Souvenir Guide and Cata

The Royal Pavilion Brighton

The Palace of King George IV

Edited by David Beevers, Keeper of the Royal Pavilion

LEFT: *Detail of the cross-section from Nash's* Views

Contents

LEFT: *George 'V after Sir Thomas Lawrence (see Catalogue no. 228, p 43)*

RIGHT: *A decorative detail from the Music Room*

Introduction

TOP: A Perspective View of the Steyne at Brighthelmstone, *by James Donowell, 1778, showing how open this part of the town was at the time of Georges first visit.*

ABOVE: The Pavilion and the Steine, *by J. Spornberg, 1796. On the far right of the Marine Pavilion stands Grove House which was subsequently demolished to make way for Nash's Pavilion.*

RIGHT: Mermaids at Brighton, *by W. Heath, 1829. Visitors are shown indulging in the healthy pleasures of sea bathing.*

Brighton and George, Prince of Wales

The Royal Pavilion has played a key role in the development of Brighton and its international reputation. Brighthelmstone (as Brighton was originally called) was transformed from a small fishing town into a fashionable resort in the mid-eighteenth century through the promotion of the therapeutic qualities of sea water, both to bathe in and to drink. The success of this cure, cleverly promoted by Dr Richard Russell, drew to Brighton members of London society, including the Duke of Cumberland, the Prince of Wales's raffish and disreputable uncle.

The Prince first visited the town shortly after coming of age in 1783, when he stayed with his uncle at Grove House on the Steine. He was prompted to visit partly by a desire to escape the constraints of the stifling court of his father and partly on the recommendation of his physicians who considered that the sea water might ease the swellings in the glands of his neck. The attractions of Brighton were not purely medicinal: the Prince enjoyed the lively company of the circle of the Duke of Cumberland, the theatre, gambling and the races.

Determined to have a house of his own outside London, he instructed Louis Weltje, his Clerk of the Kitchens and Cellars, to find a suitable modest residence. A 'respectable farmhouse' on the Steine, was rented from Thomas Kemp.

In 1786, seriously in debt and intent upon a very public display of economy, George retired to Brighton, having installed Mrs Fitzherbert, a beautiful Roman Catholic whom he had secretly (but illegally) married, in a villa nearby. The following year, his financial position resolved and his debts paid, he asked Henry Holland to transform the farmhouse. The resulting small neo-classical structure with a central domed rotunda surrounded by Ionic columns was known as the Marine Pavilion.

The Prince's presence in Brighton, and the *beau monde* who followed him, brought considerable prosperity to the local tradesmen, although his own bills were not always paid promptly. By 1800 it had become, according to the *Brighton Directory*, 'the most frequented [and] without exception one of the most fashionable towns in the Kingdom'. Over the following decades elegant town houses, squares and crescents were constructed reflecting the affluence and popularity of the town.

The Building of the Royal Pavilion: from Holland to Nash

The evolution of the Pavilion from the modest neo-classical structure designed by Henry Holland (1745–1806) in 1787 to the grand oriental design of John Nash, completed in the early 1820s, mirrors the changing status of George, Prince of Wales, from Prince Regent (1811–20) to King George IV (1820–30).

The Marine Pavilion: 1787

The Marine Pavilion consisted of the central rotunda, flanked to the south and north with two wings, all clad in cream glazed Hampshire tiles. The left (south) wing represents the location of the original farmhouse. It was not a large building. The main rooms on the ground floor comprised a breakfast room, dining room and library. In 1801–2 the Pavilion was enlarged by the architect P. F. Robinson (from Holland's office) who added a new dining room and a conservatory built at angles to the main building.

Between 1803 and 1808 a new stable block was built by William Porden in the Indian style. 'A stupendous and magnificent Building' it soon dwarfed the Marine Pavilion. It could house in elegant style some sixty horses and remains a monument to the Prince's passion for riding and racing (see p.74 in *Guide to the Royal Pavilion Estate and the Gardens*).

TOP: The Prince of Wales' Pavilion at Brighthelmstone taken from the Steyn, *by S. H. Grimm, depicting the transformation by Henry Holland of the 'respectable farmhouse' into the Marine Pavilion in 1787. The original farmhouse was incorporated into the left-hand wing of the new structure. Reproduced by permission of the British Library.*

CENTRE: A Bird's Eye View of the Pavilion, Brighton, *English School, 1817, illustrating the transformation from Holland's neo-classical building into Nash's final oriental design; the Banqueting and Music Rooms can be seen under construction, with the Great Kitchen (far left) already completed. Reproduced by courtesy of the Art Institute of Chicago.*

ABOVE: The East Front of the Pavilion *from Nash's* Views *showing the Pavilion completed; the basic form of Holland's neo-classical Pavilion is now concealed by Nash's transformations.*

Nash's Pavilion: 1815–1823

The transformation of Holland's Pavilion did not commence until 1815, by which time the Prince had become Regent, following his father's incapacitating illness. The chosen architect was John Nash (1752–1835). In proposing an Indian style for the exterior, Nash was responding to the dominance of the stable block but he was also inspired by the proposals of Humphrey Repton. In1808 Repton had had published designs for a new palace based on Indian architectural forms. An important source for both Nash and Repton was William and Thomas Daniell's four volumes entitled *Oriental Scenery*, which Nash had borrowed from the library at Carlton House for the purpose of 'making drawings for the Pavilion'.

TOP: The West Front of the Pavilion *from Nash's* Views, *illustrating Nash's completed oriental design set in a picturesque landscape.*

RIGHT: Cross-section through the Saloon's dome, *by W. Nixon, 1827. To create the great dome of the Saloon, the centrepiece of the Pavilion, Nash superimposed a cast-iron framework over Holland's building. The Bath stone minarets were also supported by iron cores, indicated in blue in Nixon's drawing. The iron frame and ribs were in place by October 1818.*

The reconstruction took some seven years, commencing with alterations to the western central front, followed by the construction of the Great Kitchen and the two new State Rooms, the Music Room and Banqueting Room. The entire building, the structure and the elaborate internal decorations, was completed in 1823.

The interior decorative scheme

The interior of the Pavilion today reflects the combined talents of the artist-designers Frederick Crace (1779–1859) and Robert Jones (active 1815–23). Crace's involvement began with the first phase of chinoiserie decoration in the Marine Pavilion 1801–2. As Nash's rebuilding commenced in 1815, so redecoration was necessary. Crace designed the new interiors, in particular the Long Gallery, the Saloon (subsequently redecorated by Jones in 1823), and the adjacent galleries.

In 1817 the Prince Regent met Crace and Jones to determine who would be responsible for which rooms; most of the major rooms were designed by Jones (the Banqueting Room, Saloon, Red Drawing Room and the King's new private apartments) while Crace undertook the new Music Room, together with the Music Room and Banqueting Room Galleries. The final schemes, with their rich and sophisticated decoration combined with the superb quality of the furniture and furnishings, created a magnificent and appropriate setting for the new monarch. The decoration is designed to increase in richness as the visitor penetrates further into the building. The decorative schemes are planned to work from the floor to the ceiling with particular emphasis being placed on dramatic forms of lighting.

Following the death of George IV the Pavilion was also used as a Royal residence first by William IV and then by Queen Victoria until 1845. In the mid 1840s Queen Victoria decided to acquire Osborne House on the Isle of Wight as a private home for her family. When the possibility of buying the Royal Pavilion from Queen Victoria was raised in the late 1840s, leading figures in Brighton recognised the importance of the building not only to the town's history but also to its economy. Prior to purchase in 1850 by the Town of Brighton, the interior was stripped of virtually all furniture and fixtures, including wallpapers, decorative features and chimney-pieces, though many original items were subsequently returned by Queen Victoria and successive monarchs. The restoration of the Pavilion commenced in the mid-nineteenth century and the programme to restore the interior to the decorative schemes approved by George IV in the early 1820s still continues today.

TOP: The Saloon, Marine Pavilion, *by T. Rowlandson, c.1789, illustrating the neo-classical formality of the first decorative scheme.*

ABOVE: The Saloon, *1815, from Nash's* Views, *illustrating Frederick Crace's chinoiserie scheme, which marked the second phase of the Saloon's decoration.*

BELOW: The Saloon, *1823, from Nash's* Views, *illustrating the final design by Robert Jones. This regal scheme reflects George's change in status from Prince Regent to King.*

Guide to the Ground Floor

ABOVE: *Detail of the* West Front of the Pavilion *from Nash's* Views *showing the* porte cochère, *where guests arrived.*

RIGHT: The Octagon Hall *from Nash's* Views, *designed by Frederick Crace.*

LEFT: *The Octagon Hall today*

The Octagon Hall

Visitors to the Pavilion, alighting from their coaches beneath the domed *porte cochère* (a covered porch for carriages), entered through the Octagon Hall. This octagonal room with its plaster ceiling resembling the interior of a tent and delicate 'peach-blossom' coloured walls was filled with light from the full-length windows, whose frames were grained in imitation of pollarded oak. Originally it was simply furnished with fret-patterned chairs in the Chinese style and a patterned buff oil cloth on the floor. The 'handsome brass enclosed stove' supplied by Cutler and Sons in 1819 was one of the few items not removed by Queen Victoria and still remains *in situ*. The interior was lit at night by a single painted glass lantern; in Nash's view of this room a portable oil lamp is shown on the stove. This was used by footmen to guide visitors after dusk.

The Octagonal Hall catalogue

1 **Dwarf Bookcase** in rosewood with gilt wood and plaster enrichments. English, 1810–20. Bequest of Sir Albert Richardson, P.R.A., in 1964. (340324)

2 **Argand lamp** in bronze with vase-shaped reservoir. Reproduced from an original by Hancock given by His Grace the Duke of Devonshire in 1991. (341303)

The Entrance Hall catalogue

3 **Pair of Elbow Chairs** in carved and painted wood. Original Pavilion furniture. English, c.1802. Lent by H.M. H.M. The Queen.

4 **Grand Piano** in rosewood inlaid in brass and supported on a gilt fluted column. It is inscribed: 'Patent Sostenente Grand, I.H.R. Mott, J.C. Mott and Company, Makers to His Majesty; Patented 1817'. Isaac H. R. Mott, inventor of the 'Sostenente' action, which was intended to improve the sustained tone of the instrument, was a musician, resident in Brighton, and played in King George IV's band. English, 1820–25 (340060)

5 **Stool** in wood carved to simulate bamboo, and partly gilt. English, c.1820. (340022)

6 **Six Chairs** in beech simulating bamboo, probably made by Elward, Marsh and Tatham; 1802–05. Presented by S. Rodgers, Esq. and J. Silverman, Esq. (340047/52)

7 **Library Table** in pollarded oak. English, c.1815. (340164)

8 **Pair of Torchères** in mahogany and bronze, inscribed 'Designed and executed by Vulliamy and Son, London, A.D. 1807'. Bought with the assistance of the N.A.C.F. and the P.G.F. in 1971. (340010/11)

9 **Pair of Candelabra** in bronze and ormolu. French, c.1815. Bought with the assistance of the P.G.F. in 1970. (340020/1)

10 **Mantel Clock** in ormolu with figures of Diana and Actaeon beside an altar on which rests a fawn. French, c.1815. (340016)

11 **Pair of Candelabra** in ormolu. French, c.1815. (340018/9)

ABOVE: *The Entrance Hall today, facing west, with the restored clerestory windows. The panelled doors to the right of the chimney-piece are false, and were installed to create a symmetrical design, as can be seen in Nash's Views (right).*

The Entrance Hall

Floor Plan B

From the Octagonal Hall guests progressed into the Entrance Hall, a cool-coloured square room, decorated by Frederick Crace with panels and banners of serpents and dragons on a pale green background. The woodwork was grained in imitation of pollarded oak; some of the original wall decorations and grained wood can still be seen today. The room was originally lit by four globe lanterns and a clerestory of glass windows painted with dragon designs in yellow and green, the latter now restored to Crace's design.

The Entrance Hall gave access on the south side to the Red Drawing Room and on the north to the private apartments of the King and his household staff. The visitor today passes into the Long Gallery through a wide doorway over which originally ran a concealed servants' staircase, which linked the north and south ends of the servants' passage. This bridge staircase enabled servants to move between the north and south ends of the Pavilion without being seen by guests.

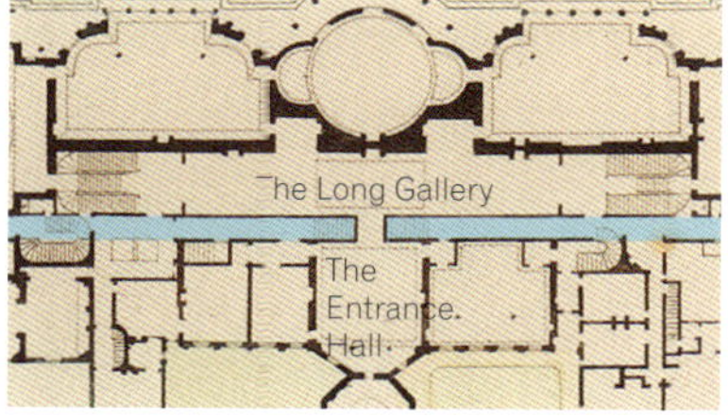

TOP: *Detail of the restored clerestory windows decorated with dragons.*

ABOVE: *Detail of a ground plan showing the location of the concealed servants' corridor and staircase, indicated in blue. Visitors will pass through a sectionof this corridor to reach the King's apartments* *(see p 41).*

BELOW: The Entrance Hall *from Nash's* Views, *designed by Frederick Crace. The restrained decoration of this reception area was intended to contrast with the drama and exuberance of the State Rooms.*

The Long Gallery

The richly decorated Long Gallery links the Entrance Hall with the Music Room and the Banqueting Room, and their galleries. As the visitor moves further into the building the decoration gets richer. Apart from linking the main State Rooms and providing access to the chamber (first) floor, the Long Gallery served as an area for playing cards, conversation or musical entertainments.

TOP: The Long Gallery *from Nash's* Views, *showing Frederick Crace's final and more formal scheme.*

ABOVE: The Long Gallery *from Nash's* Views, *c.1815: an earlier scheme designed by Frederick Crace. The niches at either side of the fireplace contained life-sized figures dressed in Mandarin robes.*

LEFT: *The Long Gallery today, furnished with some of its original furniture lent by H.M. The Queen.*

The Gallery was dramatically lit by a large, central, painted-glass ceiling or laylight. Painted laylights and windows to the north and south also illuminated the stairwells and cast-iron bamboo staircases. These features can still be seen *in situ*. In the evening the Gallery was lit with brightly painted lanterns, decorated with tassels, and a central chandelier which was transferred from the Saloon to this position in about 1821. The vertical painted windows at each end of the Gallery were illuminated from the exterior at night, by gas, suffusing the interior with soft colours. The walls of the Gallery, partitioned by bamboo fretwork, were painted with a design of rocks, trees, shrubs and birds in tones of blue on a pink background. Unfortunately, these wall decorations have not survived; the scheme today is a restoration dat ng from the 1950s. The plum-coloured, geometric-patterned carpet is a reproduction of the original design.

The interior was furnished with bamboo-pattern cabinets and pedestals, oriental jars and bottles, pagodas and Chinese figures. Some of the original bamboo furniture, on loan from H.M. The Queen, can be seen in this room. The Long Gallery exemplifies the illusion and decorative tricks so characteristic of the Pavilion: iron cast to imitate bamboo, furniture in beech simulating bamboo, painted glass laylights flanked by imitation laylights painted on canvas. Carefully placed mirrors reflected images across the gallery and when the mirror-backed doors at each end were closed 'an almost magical illusion [was] produced, the perspective appearing interminable'. (Brayley, 1838, see p.63)

ABOVE: *A Chinese Court Official, made of unfired clay, painted. Illustration reproduced by permission of H.M. The Queen.*

RIGHT: *Detail of the cast iron imperial staircase. The handrail is of mahogany carved and painted to resemble bamboo. The painted glass windows were lit from behind at night.*

Floor Plan 

The Long Gallery catalogue

12 **'The Drummer-Boy Clock'** in gilt bronze and enamel, similar to a clock made for the Prince of Wales' Chinese Drawing Room at Carlton House c.1792, which was brought to the Royal Pavilion in 1819. French, c.1880, fitted with an earlier movement by Manière. Bought with the assistance of the P.G.F. in 1985. (340316)

13 **Pair of Candlesticks** in ormolu. French, c.1830. (340025/6)

14 **Twelve Figures** standing and seated, of Chinese Court Officials, made of unfired clay, painted, Chinese, Jiaqing period (1796–1820). Four of them bought with the assistance of the P.G.F. and the N.A.C.F. in 1967 (341109/12) and eight figures lent by H.M. The Queen.

15 **Pair of Pedestals** in beech and bamboo, with panels of Spode porcelain; made for their present position in the Pavilion 1820–22. Presented by Queen Mary in 1953. (340027/8)

16 **Set of Five Cabinets** in beech, carved and painted in imitation of bamboo. From a set of six made c.1802 possibly by Elward, Marsh and Tatham for the Long Gallery. Lent by H.M. The Queen.

17 **Pair of Vases** in porcelain, with raised decoration of the 'Thousand objects of Chinese culture'. Chinese, probably Canton, c.1820. (340034/5)

18 **Six Chairs** in beech simulating bamboo, from a set made for various rooms in the Pavilion, by Elward, Marsh and Tatham in 1802. Lent by H.M. The Queen.

19 **Six Armchairs** in bamboo and canework, made in China for the European market c.1800. Three presented by the Misses Lea (340043/4 and 340303) and three lent by H.M. The Queen.

20 **Chair** in bamboo and split cane, made in China, possibly Canton, for the European market, 1800–20. Presented by Smith & Watson Inc., New York, in 1985. (340323)

21 **Occasional Table** in mahogany, turned and painted to simulate bamboo fitted with plaques of Chinese porcelain of the Jiaqing period (1796–1820). English, c.1820. Purchased with assistance of the P.G.F. in 1970. (340029)

22 **Four Chairs** in beech carved to simulate bamboo and painted green, from a set by Elward, Marsh and Tatham in 1802. Lent by H.M. The Queen.

23 **Pair of Vases** in carved red lacquer. Chinese, Jiaqing period, (1796–1820). Lent by H.M. The Queen.

24 **Games Table** in rosewood, with brass inlay and sliding chessboard. English, 1810–20. Bequeathed by Mrs A.D. Jenkins through the National Art Collections Fund in 1978. (340315)

25 **Mantel Clock** in ormolu, based on *The Oath of the Horatii,* painted in 1784 by J. L. David, now in the Louvre. A similar but larger clock was bought by the Prince of Wales for Carlton House in 1809. Purchased in 1958. (340040)

26 **Pair of Candelabra** in bronze and gilt metal. English, c.1815. (340041/2)

27 **Pair of Side Tables** in satinwood simulating bamboo, with a satinwood shelf and a black marble top with ormolu gallery. Original furniture made for the Long Gallery, possibly by Elward, Marsh and Tatham, c.1802. Lent by H.M. The Queen.

28 **Sofa Table** in rosewood and mahogany, with brass inlay. English, 1812–15. (340163)

29 **Four Elbow Chairs** in carved and painted wood. Original Pavilion furniture. English, c.1802. Lent by H.M. The Queen.

30 **Two Pairs of Cabinets** in beech simulating bamboo with yellow *scagliola* tops and brass galleries. Possibly made by Elward, Marsh and Tatham, for the Long Gallery of the Royal Pavilion, c.1802. Lent by H.M. The Queen.

31 **Pair of Incense Burners** in the form of elephants in *cloisonné* enamel with gilt and glass bead decoration, Chinese c.1800. Lent by H.M. The Queen.

32 **Two Side Tables** in beech simulating bamboo, with a rosewood top and shaped gallery. Original Pavilion furniture. English, c.1802. Lent by H.M. The Queen.

33 **Occasional Table** in bamboo and split cane with folding legs. Chinese for the European market c.1800. (340341)

34 **Four Pedestals** in beech similar to original Pavilion furniture. English, c.1820. Purchased with the assistance of the N.A.C.F., and G. Levy, Esq, in 1966. (340036/9)

35 **Large Stand** in beech simulating bamboo, octagonal with marbled pine top. Original Pavilion furniture, c.1802. Lent by H.M. The Queen

36 **Pair of 'Nubian' Figures** in the form of male and female water carriers, in carved gilt and silvered wood. Venetian, 1770–80. (340030/1)

37 **Pair of Incense Burners** in enamelled bronze in the form of the 'Dog of Fo'. Chinese, Jiaqing period (1796–1820). Lent by H.M. The Queen.

38 **Watch Stand** in ormolu on a lacquered base, in the form of a Chinese shrine. English, c.1780. (340331)

39 **Mantel Clock** in marble and ormolu in the form of a Chinese temple. The movement is probably by Pierre Gavelle of Paris. French, 1785–90. (340024)

40 **Pair of Candelabra** in bronze and ormolu. Possibly French, c.1810. (340332/3)

41 **Pair of Candlesticks** in bronze and ormolu. French, c.1810. (340334/5)

42 **Games Table** in rosewood with brass inlay. English, 1810–20. (340045)

43 **Sofa Table** in kingwood, with brass inlay and ormolu mounts. English, c.1815. (340141)

44 **Lantern Stand** carved and painted wood. Probably designed by Frederick Crace for the Long Gallery, c.1815. (340406)

The Banqueting Room

The Banqueting Room remains one of the most magnificent interiors in the Pavilion. Its imaginative and bold design was the work of Robert Jones, a little-known but extremely talented artist who began to work for the Prince Regent in 1815.

Guests, led to dine from the low-ceilinged Long Gallery or from the Banqueting Room Gallery, marvelled at the change in scale and the splendour of its decoration. As generally no more than thirty guests dined here, thirty-six plain chairs with two armchairs in ebonized wood with brass and satinwood decoration were supplied in 1817 by Bailey and Sanders; reproductions, generously provided by Smith & Watson Inc., are today displayed around the table with an original armchair, lent by H.M. The Queen.

Many elaborate banquets were held here. In 1816–17 the Prince Regent secured the services of the renowned French chef Marie-Antoine Carême who devised elaborate menus with as many as sixty dishes. Indeed, the customs and table settings found at the Prince Regent's court inspired Carême to perfect his own art to match this royal setting. Today the table is set for the dessert course with an appropriately lavish display of ormolu, candelabra and plate.

ABOVE: The Banqueting Room *from Nash's* Views, *designed by Robert Jones.*

LEFT: *The Banqueting Room today.*

TOP: *Detail of one of the original murals by Robert Jones.*

ABOVE: *One of the remaining original murals by Robert Jones showing a Chinese bridal procession.*

The interior of the Banqueting Room was designed with a shallow dome and canopies to the north and south, providing numerous arches, coves and elliptical shapes, ideal for decoration. The walls were hung with large canvases painted with Chinese domestic scenes, all of which were removed by Queen Victoria in the 1840s. Some canvases were subsequently returned, but most shown today are versions painted by the expatriate French artist Antoine Dury in 1864. From the centre of the dome hung a 30ft chandelier, a ton in weight, held in the claws of a silvered dragon suspended from the apex of the ceiling. Below, six smaller dragons exhaled light through lotus glass shades; the effect, as contemporaries observed, was 'dazzling'.

The overall scheme represented a late flowering of chinoiserie, purely decorative and theatrical in spirit. Concealed, however, within the brown and gold canopy decorations, with their complex designs of fabulous beasts, heavenly bodies and rays, are Masonic symbols. The inclusion of these symbols reflects the Prince of Wales's involvement with Freemasonry. He was the Grand Master of the Prince of Wales Lodge, constituted in 1787 (the year of the completion of the Marine Pavilion). The Prince of Wales Lodge comprised mostly his friends, who would have appreciated the significance of these symbols woven into Jones's design.

The room today is furnished with the original lampstands, made of blue jars of Spode porcelain with ormolu dragon mounts. On the window wall can be seen one of the original sideboards, on loan from H.M. The Queen, veneered in satinwood with carved and giltwood dragons. The collection of Regency silver gilt on display is the most important of its kind anywhere on public view. Together with the silver shown in the adjoining Deckers' Room, it is chiefly from the Londonderry and Ormonde Collections, two of the great aristocratic collections of the period.

The present table setting is based on an aquatint of the Banqueting Room executed c.1823 for John Nash, where the dining table is set for the dessert course. The display is a compromise between authenticity and practicality; some items which might originally have appeared on the table are placed on the sideboards, where they are more clearly visible to visitors. It was the custom in the Regency period to display with great care the host's collection of plate, as it emphasised his status and wealth. The pieces are therefore placed on the sideboards facing the light, where they are shown to best advantage.

Floor Plan D

TOP LEFT: *Detail of the dragon holding the central chandelier in the Banqueting Room. The copper leaves stand proud of the ceiling adding to the illusory effect.*

TOP RIGHT: *Detail of one of the eight original lamps designed by Robert Jones, decorated with elaborate ormolu dragon mounts.*

ABOVE: *Detail of the gilt dragons on one of the original sideboards designed for the room by Robert Jones. Illustration reproduced by permission of H.M. The Queen.*

LEFT: *The central chandelier in the Banqueting Room.*

The Banqueting Room catalogue

The Regency silver gilt on display in the Banqueting Room is the most important of its kind anywhere on public view. Together with the silver shown in the adjoining Table Deckers' Room, it is chiefly from the Londonderry and Ormonde Collections, two of the great aristocratic collections of the period.

The major portion of the Marquess of Londonderry's Collection, previously on loan to the Royal Pavilion, years was purchased in 1982 with generous aid from the Victoria and Albert Museum Purchase Grant Fund, the National Art Collections Fund, the Pilgrim Trust, and the National Heritage Memorial Fund. Amongst the Londonderry plate, many articles are from the Ambassadorial Service supplied to Sir Charles Stewart, later Baron Stewart and 3rd Marquess of Londonderry (1778–1854), in 1813. The white (silver) and gilt plate was made by Paul Storr and Benjamin Smith for the Royal goldsmiths, Rundell, Bridge and Rundell. Stewart was envoy to Berlin and ambassador to Vienna. From the 17th century ambassadors and envoys representing the Crown overseas were given an allowance of plate. In theory this was supposed to be returned at the end of the period of office, but in practice this rarely happened and the silver became their personal property. The Londonderry plate is of great historical significance because it was one of the last services to be kept as a perquisite in the customary manner. The items from the Marquess of Ormonde's collection were allocated by HM Government to the Royal Pavilion in 1982 in lieu of estate duty.

Table Plan

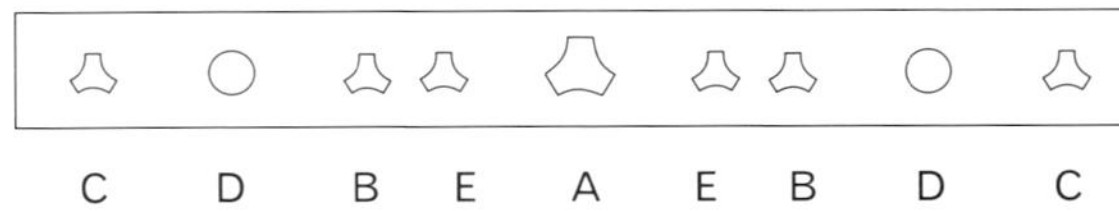

C D B E A E B D C

Displayed On The Table

To avoid visual confusion the items are not numbered. The major pieces, however, are indicated A–E, on the plan above.

A **Centre Piece** in silver gilt, in the form of a dessert-stand. Paul Storr, for Rundell, Bridge and Rundell, London, 1810. Ormonde. (344334)

B **Pair of Candelabra** in ormolu, with sphinx tripod bases supporting Egyptian figures. Bought by the Prince Regent in 1811. Lent by H.M. The Queen.

C **Pair of Candelabra** in silver gilt. Benjamin and James Smith, London, 1807. Ormonde. (344335/6)

D **Pair of Table Centres** in gilt metal. The drum-shaped base decorated with three female figures representing Fortuna, Ceres and Flora. Possibly French, c.1820. Londonderry. (344155/6)

E **Pair of Dessert Stands** in silver gilt. Robert Garrard, London, 1828. Bought with the assistance of the P.G.F. in 1979. (344169/70)

Twelve Dessert Knives, Spoons and Forks in silver gilt, from a table service engraved with the Ormonde crest, by Eley, Fearn and Chawner, the knives by Moses Brent, 1808. Ormonde. (344212/302)

Twelve Cheese Knives in silver gilt, engraved with the Ormonde crest. Moses Brent, 1808. Ormonde. (344337/48)

Twelve Dessert Knives, Forks, Spoons and Cheese Knives in silver gilt, all engraved with the crest of the Earls of Rosslyn. George Smith and others, London, from 1795–1828. Bought with the assistance of the P.G.F. in 1978. (344350/445)

Twenty-four Wine Glass Coolers in gilt metal. A glass was often inverted in crushed ice in order to keep the wine cool for longer. Engraved on each side with the Vane-Tempest crest. John Roberts & Co., c.1810. Londonderry. (344102/25)

Four Decanter Stands in silver gilt. At the base of each is engraved the Royal Coat of Arms. Benjamin and James Smith, London, 1809. Londonderry. (344129/32)

Decanter Stand similar to the above, by Digby Scott and Benjamin Smith, 1804. Londonderry. (344133)

Four Decanter Stands similar to the above, the bases engraved with the Ormonde coat of arms Benjamin Smith, London, 1808. Ormonde. (344198/201)

Pair of Decanter Stands in silver. Engraved with the Stewart crest, by Christopher Haines, Dublin, 1785–90. Londonderry. (344146/7)

Ten Wine Labels in silver gilt. Benjamin and James Smith, London, 1809–10. Londonderry. (344027/37, 344162)

Four Fruit Baskets in silver gilt. J. W. Storey and W. Elliot, London, 1811. Londonderry. (344089/92)

Fruit Basket in silver gilt, with solid centre disc engraved 'Oswestry Races 1809'. Benjamin Smith, London, 1808. Londonderry. (344154)

Dessert Service in porcelain, comprising plates, dishes and ice cream pails. Coalport. Presented by King George III to his physician, Dr Willis. English, c.1805. (341119/54)

Drinking Glasses English, possibly Stourbridge, c.1830. (340461/524)

Displayed Around The Room

45 **Four Pairs of Candelabra** in ormolu. Probably French, c.1780. Lent by H.M. The Queen.

46 **Four Wine Coolers** with liners, in gilt metal, on each side is engraved the Londonderry crest. English, c.1820. Londonderry. (344098/101)

47 **Pair of Trays** in silver gilt. Each rectangular tray is engraved with the Londonderry coat of arms. L. Valadier, Rome, 1790–1800. Londonderry. (344141/2)

48 **Six Salt-cellars** in silver gilt, with glass liners. Engraved with the Ormonde crest. Paul Storr, London, 1809. Ormonde. (344187/92)

49 **Jug** in silver gilt with hinged lid. Benjamin Smith, London, 1835. Purchased with the assistance of the Friends and the P.G.F in 1980. (344171)

50 **Pair of Side Tables** in mahogany. English, c.1810. Presented by P. Blairman Esq. (340437/8)

51 **Four Cellarets** in mahogany. English, c.1810. (340444/7)

52 **Eight Pedestal Lamps** consisting of columns of dark blue Spode porcelain flanked by ormolu dragons and with gilt brass mounts by Vulliamy on drums of wood, carved, painted and gilt, with lion-paw feet. The lamps on the window side are each supported by four carved and gilt wood dolphins. Made for the Banqueting Room to the design of Robert Jones c.1820. Presented by H.M. King George V in 1920. (340553/60)

53 **Pair of Sidetables** in mahogany. English, c.1790. (340439/40)

54 **Pair of Trays** in silver gilt, engraved with the Ormonde arms. One by Digby Scott and Benjamin Smith, London, 1804, the other by Benjamin and James Smith, London, 1809. Ormonde. (344202/3)

Floor Plan D

55 **Pair of Soup Tureens** in silver gilt, each with a silver liner and standing on an oval tray supported on lion-paw feet; on one side the Royal Arms and on the other the Stewart arms. The dragon *statant* finial on each lid is the family crest. Paul Storr, 1813 (the stands 1814). Londonderry. (344000/1)

56 **Six Wine Coolers** in silver gilt. The Royal Arms applied on one side, the Stewart arms on the other. Paul Storr, London, 1813. Londonderry. (344020/5)

57 **Pair of Dishes** in silver gilt. English, c.1810. Londonderry. (344157/8)

58 **Twenty-four Dining and two Elbow Chairs** based on the original Banqueting Room chairs made by Bailey and Sanders in 1817, reproduced exclusively for the Royal Pavilion. Presented to the Royal Pavilion by Smith & Watson Inc., New York, in association with Ferrando Guanter, S. L. Valencia in 1988. (341249/64, 341276/86)

59 **Elbow Chair** in beech simulating ebony, with satinwood details and brass inlay. One of a suite of chairs made for the Banqueting Room in 1817 by Bailey and Sanders. Lent by H.M. The Queen.

60 **Cellaret** in mahogany, of sarcophagus form with applied crocodile motif. Original Pavilion furniture. English, 1805. Presented by I. Askew, Esq., in 1986. (341238)

61 **Sideboard Cupboard** in rosewood. The form of this magnificent piece derives from designs by Thomas Hope and George Smith. English, c.1810. Presented in memory of Captain V. Bulkeley-Johnson by his widow in 1969. (340441)

62 **Candelabrum** in silver gilt, the base engraved with the Royal Arms and the Londonderry coat of arms, and the centre light surmounted by the family crest. Paul Storr, 1813. Londonderry. (344140)

63 **Sideboard Dish** in silver gilt. William Pitts, London, 1809. Ormonde. (344197)

64 **Pair of Dishes** in silver gilt. William Pitts, London, 1810 and 1817. Londonderry. (344134 and 344139)

65 **Pair of Dessert Stands** in silver gilt, engraved beneath with the Ormonde crest. Paul Storr, London, 1810. Ormonde. (344193/4)

66 **Pair of Dishes** in silver gilt. William Pitts, London, 1810. Londonderry. (344137/8)

67 **Pair of Pier Tables** mirror-backed, in mahogany, carved and gilt with ormolu mounts. Grey marble top, and shelf and marbled base. English, c.1805. (340442/3)

68 **Two Pairs of Candelabra** in ormolu. Probably French, c.1780. Lent by H.M. The Queen.

69 **Pair of Wine Coolers** in silver gilt, engraved with the Ormonde crest. Paul Storr, for Rundell, Bridge and Rundell, 1808–9. Ormonde. (344185/6)

70 **Pair of Salvers** in silver gilt, the centre engraved with the Ormonde arms. Benjamin and James Smith, London, 1808. Ormonde. (344204/5)

71 **Four Wine Coolers** in gilt metal. Engraved with the Vane-Tempest coat of arms and the covers surmounted by the Vane crest. John Roberts & Co., Sheffield, 1810–15. Londonderry. (344094/7)

72 **The Brighton Cup** for 1826 in silver gilt, engraved with the Royal Arms and inscribed 'Brighton Races 1826'. Stewards, The Earl of Egremont, The Viscount Dunwich'. John Bridge for Rundell, Bridge and Rundell, London, 1826. (344182)

73 **Cup and Cover** in silver gilt, of the Trafalgar Vase design attributed to John Flaxman. Benjamin Smith for Rundell, Bridge and Rundell, London, 1807. Bought with the assistance of the P.G.F. in 1980. (344180)

74 **Two Dessert Dishes** in silver gilt, engraved beneath with the Ormonde crest. William Fountain, London, 1809. Ormonde. (344195/6)

75 **The Brighton Cup** for 1805 in silver gilt, surmounted with the Prince of Wales' crown and feathers; on one side a panel representing the Royal Pavilion as built by Holland, on the other a figure of Victory presenting a crown to the winner of a classical horse race. John Emes for Rundell, Bridge and Rundell, London, 1805. (344181)

76 **Cup and Cover** in silver gilt. The Company of Matthew Boulton, Birmingham, 1810. Bought with the assistance of the P.G.F. in 1979. (344172)

77 **Pair of Dishes** in silver gilt, with the centres engraved with the Londonderry coat of arms. Edward Farrell, London, 1818. Londonderry. (344135/6)

78 **Pair of Urns and Pedestals** in carved mahogany intended to hold cold water. English, c.1785. (340459/60)

79 **Pair of Knife Boxes** in rosewood with boxwood and ebony inlay. English, c.1790. Acquired through the N.A.C.F. from the Ernest E. Cook Bequest, 1956. (340451/2)

80 **Sideboard** in pine and beech, veneered in rosewood and satinwood with carved and gilt dragon supports. Seven sideboards of this pattern, designed by Robert Jones and made by Bailey and Sanders in 1817, were among the original furniture of the Banqueting Room – three along the west wall, and shorter versions flanking each fireplace. The example here was modified for use in Buckingham Palace. Lent by H.M. The Queen.

81 **Centre Piece** in silver parcel-gilt, made for presentation by his regiment to Col. James Gordon of Culvennan, who is represented as the horseman on the base. Benjamin and James Smith, London, 1810. Bought with the assistance of the P.G.F. in 1978. (344183)

82 **Pair of Candelabra** in silver. The Royal Coat of Arms of George, Prince of Wales is applied to the stems. Benjamin Smith, London, 1807. Bought with the assistance of the N.A.C.F. and the P.G.F. in 1978. (344167/8)

83 **Cup and Cover** in silver gilt. Presented in 1793 to William Praed, M.P. by the Grand Junction Canal Company. John Schofield, London, 1793. Bought with the assistance of the P.G.F. in 1979. (344184)

84 **Six Dishes** from a dessert service, silver gilt; the centres engraved with the Ormonde arms. Benjamin and James Smith, London, 1810. Ormonde (344206/11)

85 **Clock** in ormolu, in the form of a garden urn surmounted by a vase. The movement is by Ancely, of Toulouse. French, 1785–90. (340454)

86 **Pair of Candelabra** in bronze and ormolu, in the style of P. P. Thomire. French, c.1810. (340455/6)

87 **Clock** in ormolu, in the form of figure symbolizing the Sciences, standing beside an altar. The movement is by Schueler, Paris. French, c.1810. (340453)

88 **Pair of Candelabra** in bronze and ormolu in the style of P. P. Thomire. French, 1815–20. (340457/8)

The Table Deckers' Room

To reach the Great Kitchen, visitors pass through this small room, also known as the Deckers' or Pages' Room. Originally furnished with glass-fronted cupboards and large mahogany tables, it functioned as a service area for the footmen, who brought in prepared dishes from the Great Kitchen to the Banqueting Room. Currently displayed here is part of the silver table service from the Marquess of Londonderry's collection.

ABOVE: The Banqueting Room *from* Nash's Views *showing the room's complex construction. Beneath the* Banqueting Room *were cellars for storing wine. The Table Deckers' (or Pages') Room can be seen on the right.*

RIGHT: *The Banqueting Room table today, set for the dessert course.*

The Table Deckers Room catalogue

89 **Sideboard** in kingwood veneer on mahogany, oak and pine, with some brass inlay; cupboard zinc-lined as a wine cooler. English, c.1810. (340561)

90 **Salver and Tea and Coffee Service** in silver gilt, consisting of kettle on spirit lamp, sugar basin, teapot, coffee pot and cream jug. The inscribed salver was a christening present (1833) from King William IV to his niece, Princess Mary Adelaide of Cambridge, mother of Queen Mary. Robert Garrard, London, from 1831–49. Purchased with assistance of the P.G.F. in 1979. (344173/8)

91 **Hot Water Urn** in silver. Richard Cooke, London, 1809. Londonderry. (344093)

92 **Coffee Urn** in copper with chased ormolu mounts. English, c.1800. (340562)

93 **Four Entrée Dishes with Covers** in silver on stands with spirit lamps, the sides applied with the Royal Arms and Stewart arms. Paul Storr, London, 1813. Londonderry. (344002/5)

94 **Four Dishes with Covers** in silver, the handles in the form of the gryphon of the Stewart crest. Paul Storr, London, 1813. Londonderry. (344011/4)

95 **Four Dishes with Covers** oval, in silver, the sides of the covers applied with the Royal Arms and the Stewart arms, and the handles in the form of the Stewart crest. Paul Storr, London, 1813. Londonderry. (344006/9)

96 **Entrée Dish and Cover** in silver; the cover with the Ormonde crest. The body engraved with the Ormonde arms. Paul Storr, London, 1807. (344332)

97 **Toasted-cheese Dish** in silver. William Stevenson, London, 1809. Londonderry. (344128)

98 **Oval Tray** in silver, engraved with the Royal Arms. Paul Storr, London, 1813. Londonderry. (344010)

99 **Inn Clock** with Chinese-style figures on a black japanned ground, and movement by Thomas Yoakley, of London. English, 1760–80. (340563)

100 **Pair of Sideboard Pedestals and Vases** in mahogany, carved in the manner of Thomas Chippendale. English, c.1770. Aquired through the N.A.C.F. in 1979. (340564/5)

101 **Set of Six Tea Canisters** decorated in the Chinese manner and bearing the stamp of T. Sutcliffe & Co, of Manchester. Nineteenth century. (340566/71)

102 **Plate Warmer** in lacquered iron, decorated with flowers in gold in the Chinese manner. The back is open so as to allow the heat of the fire to warm the plates, while the door in front retains the heat until the plates are required. English, c.1820. (340572)

103 **Royal Arms** in carved and painted wood with reeded frame, from the Captain's cabin of H.M.S. *Warspite*, 1810–20. Presented by Miss Diana Coutts. (340573)

104 **Three Cellarets** in mahogany. English, 1810–20. (340448/50)

The Great Kitchen

Floor Plan 

George IV was delighted not only with the design but also the equipment of his new kitchen, sometimes also known as the 'King's Kitchen'. Guests were escorted to inspect this room, conceived by the King as a continuation of the Pavilion's public apartments. The proximity of the new kitchens to the Banqueting Room was unusual for this period. It was more common for there to be a distance to reduce the risk of fire and smells.

The Kitchen was one of the first areas to be completed as part of John Nash's reconstruction. The main kitchen and culinary offices were erected in 1816 and the extensive cooking equipment was supplied by William Stark in 1817–18 (see p.61 for further details). A high lantern ceiling, fitted with twelve sash windows gave the spacious interior a light and airy feel. Four cast iron columns with painted copper palm leaves supported the high ceiling. Copper tent-like awnings, decorated with cast-copper ornaments, were designed to draw away the excess heat, smells and steam from the cooking range beneath. On the south wall stood a kitchen fire with smoke jack, a device for mechanically turning a spit. The strong upward draught from the kitchen fire turned a metal turbine set in the chimney and a series of gears, pulleys and chains transformed this motion to the spit. Five spits could be operated simultaneously, enabling the chef to present several roast dishes on the menu.

ABOVE: The Great Kitchen *from Nash's* Views.

LEFT: *The Great Kitchen today.*

TOP: *The smoke jack, a device for mechanically turning the spit.*

ABOVE: *Part of a batterie de cuisine, formerly the property of the Duke of Wellington and used at Apsley House. Reproduced by courtesy of the Trustees of the Museum of London.*

RIGHT: The Great Kitchen *from* Nash's Views

Here, and in the adjacent anci lary kitchens, magnificent banquets were prepared for the King. Although some of the original equipment and fittings were removed in the late nineteenth century, the interior still resembles that used by the King's team of chefs in the 1820s.

The Great Kitchen catalogue

The refurbishment of the displays in the Great Kitchen were supported by generous donations in memory of Charles Gage Esq.

105 **Collection of Copperware** comprising a set of some 550 copper utensils formerly used in the kitchen of the Duke of Wellington's London residence, Apsley House. Each piece had its own place on the shelves, the number engraved on it corresponding with the number on the shelves. Each piece also bears the ducal coronet and the letters 'D.W.L.' for 'Duke of Wellington, London'. Lent by the Trustees of the Museum of London.

A collection of thirty-nine pieces from the kitchens of the Duke of Northumberland at Syon House, Isleworth, and dated 1839, bequeathed by the Hon. Mrs Ionides (340574/612); eight pieces from the kitchen at Challenors, Rottingdean, presented by Donald Corrie, Esq. (341099/106); a kettle and fish kettle presented by Mrs Gertrude Stephens (341107/8); and a pan inscribed 'PR1817' bequeathed by Derek Sherborn in 2004. A collection of 461 items formerly in use at the National Training College of Domestic Science in London. When the College closed in 1962 the whole collection was given by the Trustees to the Royal Pavilion. (340613/1073)

106 **Pestle and Mortar** in ash and marble, with brass banding. Possibly part of the original equipment for the Great Kitchen. Lent by H.M. The Queen.

107 **Chopping Block** in oak, bound with three bands of brass. English, c.1750. Presented by Messrs. W. & F. Philbrock. (341074)

108 **Smokejack** originally powered by a rotary vane in the chimney, which was turned by the hot air rising from the fire. (341073)

109 **Four Clockwork Bottle Jacks** in brass, further devices for ensuring that meat is evenly roasted. (341095/8)

110 **Seventeen Stoneware Water Filters and Kegs** of various capacities, used for beer, cider and vinegar, many of them moulded with the Royal Arms; made by Doulton of Lambeth, c.1830. (341076/92)

111 **Bin** in salt-glazed stoneware. English, nineteenth century. (341093)

112 **Clock** in rosewood, cross-banded with mahogany, and enamel dial; part of the original fittings of the Great Kitchen. (341094)

*Visitors now return through the Banqueting Room to the **Banqueting Room Gallery**.*

Kitchen.

The Banqueting Room Gallery catalogue

113 **The Dolphin Furniture** dates from c.1810. It was commissioned by John Fish of Kempton Park, Middlesex, and it epitomises furniture with maritime motifs inspired by Nelson's victories over Napoleon at the Battle of the Nile (1798) and Trafalgar (1805). The furniture expresses the extent to which the sea had entered the national psyche; it also glorifies the Fish family name. After Fish's death in 1813, his widow presented the lamp centre piece to the Royal Hospital at Greenwich at which time it was dedicated to Lord Nelson; the rest of the furniture followed in 1815. After the closure of the Greenwich Hospital in 1869, the furniture was transferred to Admiralty House, Whitehall, where it remained until 1960. The suite is on loan from the Trustees of the Greenwich Hospital.

It comprises: sleigh-shaped settee; three window seats; backless window seat; ten arm chairs; pair of rosewood card tables with brass inlay; rosewood sofa table; pair of polescreens (fire screens). The maker of these is not known; it has been suggested that an Italian craftsman working in London may have been responsible. The centre piece (lamp or torchere) takes the form of a dolphin-supported plinth upon which is a painted vase raised above winged sphinxes in partly gilt bronze. The vase, painted possibly by Charles Muss with scenes of the Battle of Trafalgar and the Apotheosis of Nelson, is signed William Collins on the plinth. Collins was a well-known maker of mirrors, lamps and enamelled glass. The inscription reads: 'To the memory of Lord Viscount Nelson. The gift of the late John Fish Esq of Kempton Park. Presented by his widow and executrix AD 1813'.

114 **Pair of Side Tables** in rosewood with white marble tops. English c.1810. Purchased with assistance of the P.G.F. in 1961. (340063/4)

115 **Pair of Candelabra** in bronze and ormolu in the form of the winged Victory. In the style of P. P. Thomire (1751–1843). French, c.1810. (340069/70)

116 **Six Vases** in porcelain. Chinese, Jiaqing period (1796–1820). Acquired through the N.A.C.F. from the Ernest E. Cook Bequest in 1956. (340074–82)

117 **Mantel Clock** in ormolu, in the form of Cupid driving a chariot through clouds, with butterflies as steeds. French, c.1825. (340401)

118 **Pair of Candelabra** in bronze and ormolu, in the form of Cupid drawing a bow inscribed '*Garde à vous*' ('Take care'). French, c.1820. (340055/6)

119 **Table** in rosewood veneer on mahogany, with brass inlay. English, 1805–10. (340071)

120 **Sofa** in painted and gilt wood in the classical style. English, 1811–15. (340402)

121 **Pair of Side Tables** in rosewood, with brass mounted colonnettes, white marble top and mirror back. English, 1805–10. Purchased in 1969 with the assistance of the N.A.C.F. and the P.G.F.. (340061/2)

122 **Pair of Candlesticks** in bronze and ormolu on white marble bases. English, c.1800. Lent by the Regency Society of Brighton and Hove.

123 **Circular Table** in burr elm, supported by three dolphins on a triangular base with ormolu lion-paw feet. English, c. 1812. Lent by the Regency Society of Brighton and Hove.

124 **Sofa** in carved and gilt wood. English, 1810–20. (340403)

125 **Mantel Clock** in ormolu, Venus plays the lyre while Cupid holds the score. The movement is by Kinable, of Paris. French, 1780–1825. (340057)

126 **Pair of Candelabra** in ormolu. English, c.1815. (340058/9)

The Banqueting Room Gallery

Floor Plan F

This room represents the site of the original farmhouse rented by the Prince of Wales. In Holland's 1787 Marine Pavilion, it began as two rooms, an anteroom and a breakfast room. In 1815 these were combined to form the Blue Drawing Room, a name derived from an early decorative scheme by Frederick Crace. Its Regency name derives from its proximity, as a linking gallery, to the new Banqueting Room designed by Nash in c.1817.

With the remodelling by Nash of the eastern front, the bow windows of the Marine Pavilion were replaced by French windows opening on to a terrace as the room was extended to the East. The palm tree columns conceal, beneath their carved and decorative forms, cast-iron cores which support the upper floor and mark the outer limit of Holland's original building.

After dinner, guests would retire to the galleries to play cards or indulge in conversation and liqueurs. Occasionally the carpets were removed and the floors were chalked for dancing. The mood of this room was gracious and calm and provided a pause after the richness of the Banqueting Room. The walls were painted in 'flake white' with a gilt Chinese fret border. The windows and alcove recesses were furnished with a 'rich green ground satin brocade'; gilt furniture and Japanese lacquer cabinets originally graced the interior.

Today this room houses one of the finest surviving suites of Regency giltwood furniture, made to commemorate Lord Nelson and his victories, on loan from the Trustees of Greenwich Hospital.

ABOVE: *Detail of a palm tree column which conceals the cast iron core supporting the upper floors.*

ABOVE: The Blue Drawing Room, *by A. Pugin, c.1815, illustrating Frederick Crace's earlier and colourful chinoiserie scheme.*

LEFT: The Banqueting Room Gallery *from Nash's* Views *showing Frederick Crace's final and more formal decorative scheme of c.1821.*

FAR LEFT: *The Banqueting Room Gallery today.*

The Saloon

Floor Plan G

The Saloon was the central room of Holland's earlier building, and is therefore one of the oldest parts of the Pavilion. Nash preserved the physical shape of this room during his structural alterations, but the interior decoration changed several times between 1787 and 1823. It was first decorated in neo-classical style by Biagio Rebecca for Holland's Marine Pavilion. Large panels of Chinese papers and a painted sky ceiling were subsequently introduced by Frederick Crace; the interior underwent a further transformation when Robert Jones's final and opulent scheme was completed in 1823.

Jones produced a set of designs for the King that linked together every aspect of the room from floor to ceiling. The various elements were united not only by the Indian motifs used throughout, but also by the regal colour scheme. Rich white lacquer with raised gilded decoration was used for the doors, dado and free-standing furniture, whilst the richly carved frames for the great mirrors and the crimson silk panels were gilded in matt and burnished gold. A hand-knotted Axminster carpet, also designed by Jones, covered the floor, and 'His Majesty's geranium and gold colour silk' draperies furnished the windows. The final effect must have been sumptuous.

Today the carved giltwood frames are fitted with panels of hand-painted Chinese export papers, which were presented by Queen Victoria and installed in 1938. Many of the original items in the room today, including the doors at the south end of the room and the gilded pilasters and crestings, were returned to the Pavilion by Queen Victoria and later by King George V. Important free-standing pieces such as the open cabinets, made for the room by the London firm of Bailey and Sanders to Jones's design, are on loan from H.M. The Queen. The Caen stone chimney-piece, designed by John Thomas, remains *in situ*, a remnant of the refurbishment schemes of Christopher Wren Vick of 1850. At the time of writing (2009), the room is under restoration.

ABOVE: The Saloon *from Nash's* Views *showing an earlier scheme by Frederick Crace, c.1815.*

LEFT: The Saloon *from Nash'* Views, *showing Robert Jones' final scheme.*

FAR LEFT: *The Saloon today. The existing Chinese export wallpaper was returned to the Pavilion in the 1860s and hung here in 1938.*

ABOVE: *Detail of the Saloon's decoration showing Jones's use of Indian motifs.*

RIGHT: *One of the original cabinets, designed by Robert Jones, which echoes the Indian motifs used elsewhere in the room. Illustration reproduced by permission of H.M. The Queen.*

FAR RIGHT: The Saloon *from Nash's* Views *showing Nash's use of a cast iron frame to support the central dome.*

The Saloon catalogue

127 **Two Pairs of Open Cabinets** in carved, painted and gilt wood with ormolu enrichments, ormolu mounts and foliate cresting. The larger pair has a central arch of Indian design. This remarkable set, designed for the Saloon, where they were *en suite* with the chimney-piece (now at Buckingham Palace), was made between 1818 and 1823 by the firm of Bailey and Sanders, of London, to the design of Robert Jones. Lent by H.M. The Queen.

128 **Pair of Urns** in bronze and ormolu, on red marble bases. French, c.1805. (340383/4)

129 **Male Figure** in Shiwan stoneware, decorated with coloured enamels. Chinese, Canton, c.1880. (340385)

130 **Pair of Side Tables** in gilt wood, with white marble tops, possibly designed by James Moore Sr. English, c.1730. (340108/9)

131 **Pair of Urns** in ormolu and brass; the square base and marble plinth have foliate mounts. English, c.1805. (340112/3)

132 **Four Stools** in carved and gilt beech in the form of a shell with dolphin support. English, c.1812. (340087/90)

133 **Pair of Candelabra** in ormolu, one with the figure of Apollo, the other with Victory, the cylindrical plinth of malachite. Probably French, c.1810. (340085/6)

134 **Pair of Urns** on stands, in red marble, with ormolu mounts. English, c.1800. (340386/7)

135 **Female Figure** in earthenware, wearing decorative draperies and holding a small perfume bottle. Chinese, c.1820. (340390)

136 **Pair of Vases** in porcelain. Chinese, c.1780. (340387/8)

137 **Pair of Console Tables** with porphyry tops and rosewood stands. English, c.1730. Rosewood base and mirror back added in the Regency period. (340091/2)

138 **Pair of Urns** in red and cream marble, with ormolu mounts. French, c.1810. (340110/1)

139 **Carpet** in the Chinese style. English, made at Wilton nineteenth century. (340107)

140 **Mantel Clock** in the form of an Urn and a Pair of Candelabra for eight lights in grey marble with ormolu mounts, the movement signed '*Janvier à Paris*'. French, c.1850. (340104/6)

141 **Four Elbow Chairs** in carved and gilt oak with scroll arms and scimitar legs, probably made to designs of Henry Holland (architect of the Royal Pavilion of 1787). This set was made for Sir William Lee, probably for Colworth House, Bedfordshire, but were later moved to Hartwell House, Buckinghamshire, another family property. English, 1796–1800. Purchased with assistance of the P.C.F. in 1957. (340093/100)

142 **Pair of Footstools** in gilt beech in the form of the Greek console, with pine-cone feet, after a design by Matthew Gregson. English, c.1815. (340101/2)

143 **Pair of Urns** of similar design and date to No. 1378 but with lion feet and a band of fruiting vine below the lip. English, c.1800. (340391/2)

144 **Male Figure** in earthenware, wearing a decorative robe and carrying a rod. Chinese, c.1850. (340395)

145 **Pair of Vases and Covers** in porcelain decorated in *famille noire* enamels. Chinese, c.1850. (340393/4)

146 **Couch** in the form of an Egyptian river boat on crocodile feet, in painted, carved and gilt wood. English, 1806–10. Purchased for the Royal Pavilion by public subscription with the assistance of M. Trevor-Venis, Esq. and the N.A.C.F. in 1969 to honour the work of Clifford Musgrave, former Director of the Royal Pavilion. (340033/4)

147 **Vase** in porcelain. Chinese, 1650–70. (340396)

Salon.

The Music Room Gallery catalogue

148 **Pair of Pier Tables** in gilt wood with *scagliola* tops. English, 1812–15. (340377/8)

149 **Pair of Candelabra** in bronze and ormolu, with the figure of Victory upholding branches based on a hunting horn design. Possibly French, c.1810. (340118/9)

150 **Five Plain and Two Elbow Chairs** from a set in black-painted wood with gilt details. English, c.1810. (340148/53 and 340160)

151 **Pair of Side Tables** in painted and gilt wood with white marble tops. English, 1810–20. (340115/6)

152 **Six Elbow Chairs** painted and gilt with hocked-hoof arm supports. English, c. 1810. Lent by H.M. The Queen.

153 **Circular Table** in rosewood decorated with brass inlay and ormolu mounts. English, 1815–20. (340382)

154 **Pair of Couches** in rosewood inlaid with brass. English, c.1812. (340135/6)

155 **Two Pairs of Elbow Chairs** in carved and gilt beech. They are similar to chairs at Hartwell House in Buckinghamshire designed by Henry Holland. Two are branded 'H.R.', possibly the mark of Hugh Richards (1784–1827). The other two are branded 'I.M.'. English, 1800–05. Presented by Mrs B. H. Lofts-Constable in 1971. (340120/3)

156 **Sofa Table** in kingwood with satinwood veneer, with folding leather-covered top. English, c.1820. (340053)

157 **Pair of Candlesticks** in bronze and ormolu with bases of white marble. English, c.1800. (340133/4)

158 **Pair of Pier Tables** with mirror backs, in rosewood with brass inlay, cast brass colonnette supports, green marbled top and marbled wood plinth. English, c.1815. (340165/6)

159 **Pair of Female Figures** in Dehua porcelain from Fujian province, probably representing Guanyin, the maternal goddess. Chinese, c.1700. (340367/8)

160 **Four Candelabra** in chiselled, matted and burnished ormolu, of foliate form, for five lights each, supported on hexagonal Chinese porcelain columns. The candelabra were designed and made for their present position, probably by Robert Jones, in 1821. Lent by H.M. The Queen.

161 **Mantel Clock** in ormolu in the form of Apollo with his lyre by an altar. French, 1800–10. (340132)

162 **Pair of Candelabra** in patinated bronze and ormolu, with fluted columns on a Wedgwood-style base with figures in white on a blue ground. English, c.1820. (340128/9)

The Music Room Gallery

163 **Pair of Covered Vases** in porcelain of the Qianlong period, (1736–95). Chinese with French ormolu mounts of c.1770. Acquired through the N.A.C.F. from the Ernest E. Cook Bequest, in 1956. (340161/2)

164 **Writing Table** in ebony, with elaborate brass inlay and tooled leather top. Made c.1815 by Louis Le Gaigneur, cabinet-maker to the Prince Regent. Purchased 1985 with the assistance of The Coral Samuel Charitable Trust and the N.A.C.F.. (340322)

165 **Sofa Table** in calamander wood, with brass and ebony inlay. English, c.1818. (340033)

166 **Pair of Candlesticks** in the form of foliate ormolu columns on octagonal bronze bases, hung with cut crystal drops. English, 1820. (340370/1)

167 **Chair** in mahogany, with high back and revolving needlework seat. English, 1840–50. Bequest of Miss Ruby Cleeve. (340145)

168 **Grand Piano** by Isaac Mott & Co., c.1830. The case, probably supplied by Thomas Parker, is inlaid with figures of music and dancing probably derived from Thomas Hope's *Costume of the Ancients* (1809). Presented by Queen Mary in 1930. (340114)

169 **Vase** in porcelain with wooden cover. Chinese, c.1800 (340379)

170 **Table** in rosewood veneer on mahogany, with brass inlay. English 1812–15. (340117)

171 **Sofa Table** in rosewood. English, c.1820. (340381)

172 **Pair of Candlesticks** in ormolu and bronze; in the form of winged sphinxes on opal glass cylinders. English, c.1810. (340142/3)

173 **Circular Table** made as a pair to No.157, with brass inlay. English, 1815–20. (340009)

174 **Chair** from a set in beech carved and painted to simulate bamboo. Original Pavilion furniture. English, c.1805. Lent by H.M. The Queen.

175 **Two Pairs of Candlesticks** in cut crystal in the form of two urns hung with drops. English, c.1830. (340364/5 & 340374/5)

Like the Banqueting Room Gallery to the South of the Saloon, this room provided repose and calm after the grandeur of the main State Rooms. The room would have been used for small concerts and recitals; the Brussels-weave carpet was removed on occasion to allow the floor to be chalked for dancing.

An earlier bright yellow chinoiserie scheme was replaced in 1821 with a more refined and dignified scheme of 'flake white' walls with gilt decoration, both designed by Frederick Crace. It was furnished with magnificent French and English furniture, some brought down from Carlton House in London. Most of the original furniture is now at Buckingham Palace and Windsor Castle, apart from the four lampstands of Chinese porcelain and ormolu placed in the windows, on loan from H.M. The Queen. The grand piano, in a rosewood case inlaid with brass, was presented to the Pavilion by Queen Mary and is similar to the original piano that stood in this room in the Regency period.

ABOVE: The Yellow Drawing Room, *by A. Pugin, c.1815, illustrating Frederick Crace's earlier design which combined the traditional print room format with colourful chinoiserie decorations.*

LEFT: The Music Room Gallery *from* Nash's Views *illustrating Frederick Crace's final decorative scheme of 1821.*

FAR LEFT: *The Music Room Gallery today.*

The Music Room

Floor Plan 0

One of George IV's great passions was music and appropriately the second extension in Nash's scheme (in addition to the Banqueting Room, devoted to another of his pleasures) took the form of the Music Room. In this extraordinary interior, lit by nine lotus-shaped chandeliers, the King's own band entertained guests with selections from Handel or Italian opera. The Italian composer Rossini visited the Pavilion in 1823 and performed for the King. George himself would contribute to the evening's entertainment with popular airs, accompanying himself on the pianoforte.

This room remains the most significant monument to one of the King's chief decorators, Frederick Crace. Similar in structure to the Banqueting Room at the south end, the walls were decorated with painted canvases by Crace and Henry Lambelet (1781–1860). These paintings consist of Chinese scenes in rich reds heightened with gold incorporating scenes from William Alexander's *The Costume of China*, published in 1805. Painted dragons held up these canvases, just as the 'carved silvered and tinted flying dragons' supported the blue silk-satin window draperies, fringed with gold tassels. Red was used by Crace to great decorative effect

ABOVE: *Copy of the Rock Clock completed in 2001. The original, in Buckingham palace, is French, c.1735, and was sent to Brighton in 1819.*

LEFT: The Music Room *from* Nash's Views. *A concert is in progress and George IV is seated on the left with his mistress, Lady Conyngham.*

BOTTOM LEFT: The South Gate of the City of Ting-Hai *from William Alexander's* Costume of China, *1805.*

BOTTOM RIGHT: *Detail of the Music Room mural showing Crace's adaptation of William Alexander's illustration.*

FAR LEFT: *The Music Room restored following the fire of 1975.*

FROM TOP TO BOTTOM:

Firemen tackling the blaze on the night of 2 November, 1975. Reproduced by courtesy of the Evening Argus.

A conservator restoring the cove following the fire of 1975.

A copy of Crace's original mirror frame being carved in limewood in the conservation workshops.

The cove damaged by the stone ball dislodged by the hurricane in 1987.

TOP RIGHT: *The charred east wall of the Music Room after the fire in 1975.*

RIGHT: *The restored central chandelier.*

in the doors, enriched with carved and gilt elements. Gilding was also used on the cockle-shells of the domed ceiling to create an illusion of height; this was achieved partly by the size of the cockle-shells diminishing towards the apex, and partly by changing the tones of the gilding.

Tragically this splendid room was severely damaged by fire in 1975, although all but one of the original wall paintings (which were returned by Queen Victoria in the 1860s) survived. After a decade of intensive work, the restoration of the gilt dome, coving, clerestory windows and their surrounds, east wall and chandeliers was completed. The windows have been furnished with continuous draperies in silk satin, meticulously made up following original designs. The reinstatement of the curtains was made possible with generous assistance from the Leche Trust and private sponsors.

For the first time since the period of Royal occupation the Music Room has been furnished with a hand-knotted and fitted carpet. Reconstructed using evidence from surviving fragments, documents and illustrations, it faithfully reproduces the original magnificent Axminster carpet.

As part of a long-term programme of copying fixtures removed by Queen Victoria in the late 1840s, the magnificent mirror frame has also been reconstructed in carved and gilt limewood. A reproduction of the grand statuary marble fireplace (originally designed by Robert Jones and carved by Sir Richard Westmacott), replaces the original, now in Buckingham Palace.

The restoration of the interior was barely completed when the hurricane of October 1987 dislodged a stone ball on top of one of the minarets which then fell through the newly-restored ceiling, embedding itself in the newly-laid carpet. After further works by the Pavilion conservation team the room has now been restored to Crace's original scheme.

The Music Room catalogue

Organ, the original by Lincoln was removed in 1848 and installed in the Ballroom at Buckingham Palace. The present organ, also by Lincoln, was made in 1822 for the Royal Chapel at Brighton. It was returned by Queen Victoria and installed here in 1851; it has been extensively altered and modified.

Clock, this close copy of the 'Rock Clock', which originally stood here and is now at Buckingham Palace, was carved by John Powell, Senior Conservation Officer and generously sponsored by the Regency Society of Brighton and Hove in 2000.

Pair of Porcelain Pagodas, Chinese, Jiaqing (1796–1820). Purchased from Kenneth Clark with the assistance of the N.A.C.F. in 1950. (341300/1)

Floor Plan J

Before entering the King's Apartments, visitors walk through the servants' passage, decorated with tin-glazed earthenware tiles.

The King's Apartments

In Nash's remodelling the King's bedroom was moved from the first floor to the ground floor for ease of access; the king was by now hugely overweight and afflicted with gout and dropsy. The new Apartments looked out across the western lawns through French windows and a loggia to the stables and riding school, linked to the Pavilion by an underground passage for days of inclement weather.

The King's Apartments comprised a bathroom, bedroom, dressing room, library and anteroom. These private rooms were intended for comfort and convenience rather than public display and so were decorated in a more restrained style. Designed by Robert Jones, the walls were covered with a printed green-ground example of the dragon paper, first used in a hand-painted version in the Red Drawing Room. The original paper was removed by Queen Victoria and there now hangs a hand-painted version executed by Roy Bradley, an artist-restorer working in the 1950s. A reproduction of the original Brussels carpet was laid in 1994.

All these rooms were decorated *en suite*, some with ceilings painted with clouds. In the library, shelves were built into the recesses to house the King's own collection of books. As originally conceived, the rooms were furnished with a mixture of objects of different styles and epochs. This was characteristic of George's taste, with French and English furniture and Japanese lacquer combining to create an atmosphere of quiet elegance.

ABOVE: The Private Library *from Nash's* Views, *designed by Robert Jones.*

LEFT: *The King's Library today, furnished with a Brussels carpet reproducing Jones' original design.*

The King's Apartments: Bedroom catalogue

176 **Dressing Table and Writing Desk** combined, in cedar decorated with black and gold lacquer, with a folding top concealing thirteen compartments. This very rare piece, of Chinese workmanship inspired by English designs, incorporates various design elements from 'Buroe-Dressing-Tables' shown in Thomas Chippendale, *The Gentleman and Cabinet-Maker's Director*, published from 1755 onwards. Chinese, 1790–1800. Purchased with assistance of the F.G.F. in 1956. (340300)

177 **Pair of Cabinets** in satinwood incorporating Chinese lacquer panels. English 1790–1800. Lent by H.M. The Queen.

178 **Chair** in beech simulating bamboo from a set made for various rooms in the Pavilion by Edward, Marsh and Tatham, 1802. (341115)

179 **Giltwood State Bed** made for George IV's bedroom at Windsor Castle by Morrel and Seddon in 1828. The footboard, which originally supported a clock, is carved with the Royal Arms. The bed incorporated a mechanism which allowed it to be raised and lowered in response to the king's increasing infirmity. George IV died on 26 June 1830 at 3.15am on a low couch placed next to this bed. His last words were: 'My boy, this is death'. Lent by HM The Queen.

180 **Two Chairs** in beech carved and painted to simulate bamboo, from a set made by Elward, Marsh and Tatham for the Pavilion in 1802. Lent by H.M. The Queen.

181 **Armchair** beech, carved and painted to simulate bamboo, made by Elward, Marsh and Tatham for the Pavilion in 1802. Lent by H.M. The Queen.

182 **Dressing Table and Washstand** in beech carved and painted in imitation of bamboo, with rosewood top and gallery. Original Pavilion furniture. English, c.1802. Lent by H.M. The Queen.

183 **Side Table** in beech simulating bamboo with rosewood top and gallery. Original Pavilion furniture. English, c.1802. Lent by H.M. The Queen.

184 **Bedsteps** in beech, carved to imitate bamboo, and fitted with a locker. English, c.1810. (340299)

185 ***Bonheur-du-jour*** in black lacquer decorated in gold, with doors, a fitting for a watch above and for a workbag below. Elements derive from English furniture of the late-seventeenth and early-eighteenth century. Chinese, 1825–30. Lent by H.M. The Queen.

186 **Covered Urn** on a square plinth, carved in 'Blue John' (fluorspar). English, 1800–20. (340428)

187 **Chair** carved to simulate bamboo and painted to resemble black lacquer. Original Pavilion furniture, c.1802. Lent by H.M. The Queen.

188 **Firescreen** in the Chinese style, in carved, turned, painted and gilt wood. English, c.1840. Lent by H.M. The Queen.

189 **Mantel Clock** in bronze, in the form of a lyre on a rectangular base with an ormolu movement. French, c.1825. (340017)

190 **Pair of Candelabra** in ormolu and bronze. French, c.1810. (340307/8)

191 **Pair of Candlesticks** cast as a fluted column with foliate decoration in chased, gilt and burnished brass. English, 1810–15. (340297/8)

192 **Occasional Table** in bamboo, made in China for the European market, c.1800 Lent by H.M. The Queen.

193 **Card Table** in rosewood, with tassel-top legs; original Pavilion furniture. English, c.1820. Purchased with the assistance of the Friends, and the N.A.C.F. in 1974. (340296)

The King's Apartments: Library catalogue

Books: seventeenth to nineteenth century volumes, on loan from Brighton Library.

194 **Candelabrum** in ormolu, for seven lights: signed P. P. Thomire, Paris. French, c.1810. (340290)

195 **Secretaire** in rosewood with ormolu mounts in classical taste, in the French fall-front form. Probably by S.Jamar of London and Liverpool, c.1810–20. Purchased in 1962. (340288)

196 **Sofa** in faux rosewood and gilt wood, in the French style. English, c.1812. (340288)

197 **Library Steps** in mahogany, convertible to an elbow chair,the steps covered in green tooled leather. An example of the 'Patent Metamorphic Library Chair' made by Morgan & Sanders, of London. English, c.1810. (340280)

198 **Pair of Busts** of George IV and William IV in bronze. English, c.1830. Presented by Mrs Gertrude Stephens. (340286/7)

199 **Pair of Urns** in ormolu, on a square base and plinth. English, c.1810. (340276/7)

200 **Mantel Clock** in ormolu and red marble. English, c.1810. (340283)

201 **Pair of Candelabra** in marble and ormolu. English, 1800–05. (340284/5)

202 **Pair of Bookcases** in beech carved and painted in imitation of bamboo, with rosewood tops and an ormolu gallery. English, c.1805. Lent by H.M. The Queen.

203 **State Armchair** with high concave back, the front supports carved as winged sphinxes and painted in simulated bronze inlaid with gold. Probably Italian, 1808–12. Lent by the Regency Society of Brighton and Hove.

204 **Pair of Library Globes** one celestial and the other terrestrial, with framework, support, and splay feet, in light mahogany carved with formal foliage, and the bearings in brass. The celestial chart is inscribed: 'Newton's new celestial globe … on which all the fixed stars, nebulae and clusters … are laid down; the position of the whole having been recalculated for the year 1830 by W. Newton'; the terrestrial is inscribed and dated 1822. (340281/2)

205 **Pen Tray** in brass and tortoise-shell inlay on ebonised wood, brass-bound; the brass covers of the two inkwells are marked 'Parkins & Cotto, London' with royal crown in the centre. English, 1815–20. (340275)

206 **Inkstand** in silver gilt; a triangular base, with a palm tree flanked by the figures of Homer, Virgil and Milton, and between them three crowned inkwells. The whole is surmounted by the winged Victory. This piece was probably made for George IV, to serve as a gift to Lady Conyngham or to her husband, by Philip Rundell, of Rundell, Bridge and Rundell in 1821. Purchased with the assistance of the N.A.C.F. in 1963. (340274)

207 **Library Table** in dark mahogany. English, c.1800. (340273)

208 **Pair of Elbow Chairs** in mahogany, of a form based on the 'curule', derived from a design by Thomas Hope. One marked B. Harmer. English, c.1807. Presented by the Edward James Foundation in 1971. (340014/5)

209 **Settee** in mahogany with brass inlay, in the Egyptian style. English, c.1815. (340279)

210 **Chest** for maps and plans in mahogany with a green tooled-leather top. English, c.1800. Purchased in 1959. (340266)

Floor Plan J

211 **Pair of Elbow Chairs** in imitation rosewood, based on a design by Thomas Hope. One has the label of James Newton, upholsterer and cabinet maker, of 63 Wardour Street, London, recorded as working from 1790 to 1803; the other appears to read 'Albert Rawlins', an unrecorded name, and the date '1806 October 6'. Purchased with the assistance of the P.G.F. in 1956. (340418/9)

212 **Library Steps** with four treads and an upright support carved to resemble bamboo. English, 1800–20. (340425)

213 **Sofa Table** in rosewood on four bow-shaped supports, which also form the legs. English, 1810–20. Bequest of Mrs A. D. Jenkins through the N.A.C.F., in 1978. (340310)

214 **Waste Paper Basket** in woven split bamboo, brass bound. c.1825. (340309)

The King's Apartments: Anteroom catalogue

215 **Pair of Wall Lights** in carved, ebonised and gilt wood; for four lights, of Graeco-Egyptian form based on designs by Thomas Hope. English, c.1807. Bequest of Sir Albert Richardson, P.R.A. in 1964. (340255/6)

216 **Mantel Clock** in bronze, ormolu and dark red marble, in the Egyptian style. The prototype was made to the design of Thomas Hope (1769–1831) for the 'Flaxman' room of his house in Duchess Street, London. French, c.1807. Bought with the assistance of the P.G.F. in 1966. (340252)

217 **Four Elbow Chairs** from a set of ten, painted black and parcel-gilt. The set is based on a design by George Smith and was subsequently used to furnish the Tapestry Room at Forde Abbey, Dorset. English, c.1806. Purchased with the assistance of the P.G.F. in 1971. (340268/71)

218 **Pair of *Torchères*** in carved, ebonised and gilt wood in the form of a column supported by three Egyptian women. Swedish, probably made by Pehr Ljung of Stockholm (1743–1819), 1800–10. (340412/3)

219 **Pair of Candelabra** in bronze and ormolu, with the winged Victory. French, 1800–10. (340263/4)

220 **Pair of Ornaments** in bronze and ormolu, deriving from the Graeco-Roman 'Venus Anadyomene' and a figure of Cupid. French, 1795–1800. (340253/4)

221 **Side Cabinet** in calamander wood veneer with elaborate brass inlay taken from designs by George Bullock (1777–1818). English, c.1818. (340265)

222 **Mantel Clock** the ormolu base supporting a plinth and column of dark red marble in which the movement is set. The bronze figures represent Cupid and Psyche. English, c.1820. (340267)

The Yellow Anteroom catalogue

House Organ in mahogany, satinwood and rosewood with decoration in marquetry, signed by James Hancock as 'Organ builder to His Majesty' and dated 1788. This organ was found in the tower of the Roman Catholic church of St Mary, Brighton, and may have belonged to Mrs Fitzherbert. Presented by C. Rosling, Esq, in 1955.

223 **Two Elbow Chairs** in beech, carved and painted in the Chinese style. Original Pavilion furniture. English, c.1802. Lent by H.M. The Queen.

ABOVE: *George IV's State Bed (no. 179).*
Royal Collection © 2009. Her Majesty Queen Elizabeth II.

224 **Paintings** (a changing selection) in watercolour and bodycolour, probably details cut from larger sheets of hand-painted wallpaper, depicting rural scenes, exported from China to Europe, c.1800.

225 **'The Feast of the Dragon'** painted in watercolour and bodycolour, Chinese from the Canton district in c.1820. (102812)

226 **Portrait of Louis Weltje** (1745–1800) in pastel, after John Russell, R.A. (1745–1806). Weltje, the Prince's agent and later 'Clerk to the Prince of Wales' Kitchen', accompanied him to Brighton in 1784, and later bought the land on which the Pavilion stands. (100843)

227 **Portrait of John ('Old Smoaker') Miles** in pastel by John Russell, R.A. (1745–1806). Miles was bathing attendant to the Prince of Wales. (100842)

228 **Micro-Mosaic Portrait of George IV** after Sir Thomas Lawrence. Made by Domenico Moglia in the Vatican workshops in Rome using some 500,000 pieces, at the request of Pope Pius VIII, in 1828. (330331)

*Visitors now pass through the **Yellow Anteroom** and ascend the **North Staircase***

The North Staircase and Galleries catalogue

229 **Pair of Urns** in porcelain. Chinese, c.1800. (340407/8)

230 **Two Hexagonal Stands** in bamboo, one with black top, the other with *scagliola* top and brass gallery. Original Pavilion furniture, c.1800. Lent by H.M. the Queen.

231 **Two Chairs** in beech simulating bamboo, from a set made for various rooms in the Royal Pavilion, probably by Bailey and Sanders, c.1815. Lent by H.M. the Queen.

232 **Five Argand Lamps** in bronze, with vase shaped reservoir. Reproduced with assistance from the Regency Society of Brighton and Hove in 1994, from an original by Hancock given by his Grace the Duke of Devonshire in 1991. (341309/10)

233 **Occasional Table** in beech simulating bamboo, with octagonal scagliola top. English, c.1800. Lent by H.M. The Queen.

The Lobby to The Adelaide Tea room catalogue

'HRH The Prince Regent Awakening the Spirit of Brighton' painted in oil on wallpaper on the wall of a house in Preston Park, by Rex Whistler (1905–44) in 1944 whilst billetted in Brighton. Purchased with the assistance of the N.A.C.F. in 1945. (000017)

Guide to the First Floor

The North-West Gallery and Adelaide Corridor

The North-West Gallery houses a display on the history of the restoration of the Royal Pavilion which was made possible with help from the Dmitro Trust, and Rex Whistler's renowned picture, *H.R.H. The Prince Regent Awakening the Spirit of Brighton.*

Light Levels

For reasons of conservation the light levels on the first floor have been reduced in order to protect the vulnerable works of art and textiles exhibited in these areas.

The Adelaide Corridor Chinese Paper

The hand-painted Chinese wallpapers in the Adelaide Corridor are the remnants of several sets of paper acquired by George IV in 1815 and hung in this part of the Pavilion, c.1820. They probably date from the second half of the eighteenth century and may previously have been hung elsewhere, their original height having been much reduced to fit the dimensions of the corridor.

They are unique in being the only original Chinese papers left *in situ* in the building and have survived despite the physical wear and tear of a domestic area, and the harmful effects of varnishing in the Victorian period.

The panoramic landscapes are filled with hunting scenes, processions of large figures, and a dragon boat festival over which the eight immortal Taoist gods preside.

ABOVE: *Detail of the original Chinese paper in the Adelaide Corridor.*

To the left of the North Gallery visitors will find the ***Yellow Bow Rooms****, and to the right access to the* ***Queen Adelaide Tearoom*** *(marked '****C****' on Floor Plan) and the* ***Adelaide Corridor*** *adjacent.*

The Yellow Bow Rooms

The Yellow Bow Rooms, formerly the bedrooms of George IV's brothers, the Duke of York and Duke of Clarence, are locatec on the eastern front, off the North Gallery.

The design of these rooms, by Robert Jones, derives from an early scheme used in the Red Drawing Room, a room to the south of the Entrance Hall. In the Red Drawing Room the walls were hand-painted with a design of dragons, phoenixes and birds of paradise in white on brilliant carmine red to which were applied twenty-six Chinese export paintings with *trompe l'oeil* bamboo frames. George IV was so taken with this design by Jones that he commissioned him to produce a block-printed version of the wallpaper, which was used with a green background in his new ground floor apartments (see p 41) and in chrome yellow in these bedrooms. The Yellow Bow Room (north), used by the Duke of York, was decorated with Chinese oil paintings; the Yellow Bow Room (south) used by the Duke of Clarence (later William IV) was decorated with watercolours.

As part of the restoration programme for the first floor this suite of rooms, comprising a lobby, two bedrooms and servants' rooms, has been refurbished to Jones's original scheme. The dragon paper and dado have been meticulously reproduced, using as a source some original fragments. Wood blocks were cut, from which the design was hand

ABOVE: The Red Drawing Room *from Nash's* Views *showing the first use of the dragon wallpaper designed by Robert Jones with applied Chinese export paintings in their trompe l'oeil bamboo frames.*

LEFT: *The Yellow Bow Room (North) furnished with a satinwood bed. The red vase and flower chintz draperies were reconstructed using an original James Arrowsmith design of c.1819.*

ABOVE: *Detail of the north wall of the Yellow Bow Room (south) today with Jones' original scheme reinstated.*

TOP: *The dragon wallpaper being hand-printed by John Perry & Co.*

printed in the traditional manner by one of the few firms still able to do this, John Perry & Co. Twenty-four large blocks are needed for one repeat of the dragon pattern which is 12ft. by 10ft., and eight different colour blocks make up the intricate fret dado. Both designs were printed on a chrome yellow ground.

Chrome yellow, the ground colour in this scheme, was not commercially available before 1818, and so was, at the time, an innovative and modern choice; it dramatically sets off the rich and intense colouring of the Chinese oils and watercolours. The windows and beds are furnished with a 'red vase and flower chintz' which has been most generously reproduced by G.P. & J. Baker Ltd. from an original Regency fabric which survived in their archives. The mattresses for the beds have been hand-made by Heal & Son Limited to the original designs. The floor covering, as throughout the chamber floor, is a flat-weave Brussels carpet 'drab and flowers', a repeat-pattern floral design which can also be seen in the South Galleries. This has been reproduced in 27in. strips, which are then sewn together. The rooms are furnished with satinwood and mahogany furniture, some on loan from H.M. The Queen.

The restoration of these rooms could not have been undertaken without the generous support of the L. J. Skaggs and Mary C. Skaggs Foundation, The Coral Samuel Charitable Trust and The Regency Society of Brighton and Hove.

On leaving the Yellow Bow Rooms visitors cross the ***North Gallery*** *to a small exhibition room and* ***Queen Victoria's apartments****.*

The Yellow Bow Room (North) catalogue

234 **Pair of Hat Boxes** in laquered and gilt wood, made in China for the Prince of Wales, c.1800. Lent by H.M. The Queen.

235 **Pillar Table** in rosewood inlaid with brass. Original Pavilion furniture. English, c.1815. Purchased with the assistance of The Coral Samuel Charitable Trust, the P.G.F. and the Friends in 1979. (340372)

236 **Side Cabinet** in satinwood and purple wood fitted with shelves and bronze mounts. Original Pavilion furniture. English, c.1805. Bought with the assistance of the P.G.F., the N.A.C.F., and the Friends in 1993. (341294)

237 **Bed** in satinwood, English, c.1800. The mattresses were hand-made by Heal and Son Ltd. Lent by H.M. The Queen.

238 **Dressing Table** in mahogany with two drawers. English, c.1830. Lent by H.M. The Queen.

239 **Cheval Mirror** in mahogany. English, 1810–20. (340434)

240 **Arm Chair** in beech carved and painted to simulate bamboo. Probably made by Elward, Marsh and Tatham for the Pavilion in 1802. Lent by H.M. The Queen.

241 **Four Chairs** in beech simulating bamboo, from a set made for various rooms in the Royal Pavilion, probably by Bailey and Sanders, c.1815. Lent by H.M. The Queen.

242 **Pair of Lamps** in bronze and brass, urn-shaped reservoirs on cylindrical plinths. Made by Perry and Co. English, c.1820. Purchased with assistance from Christopher Howe and the P.G.F. in 1992. (341290/1)

243 **Argand Lamp** in bronze, with vase-shaped reservoir, by Hancock. English, c.1820. Given by His Grace The Duke of Devonshire in 1991. (341272)

244 **Argand Lamp** in bronze, with vase-shaped reservoir. Reproduced with assistance from The Regency Society of Brighton and Hove in 1994, from an original by Hancock, given by His Grace the Duke of Devonshire in 1991. (341304)

245 **Eighteen Paintings** in oil depicting Chinese scenes of domestic life, some of which originally hung in this room. Exported from China to Europe c.1800. (000247/55, 000622/3, 001110/1). Five are reproductions painted by Gordon Grant in 1991–92. Four of these overlap the jib doors and the fifth hangs top left of the bed.

LEFT: *Detail of the cross-section from Nash's* Views *illustrating the Yellow Bow Rooms located above the Music Room Gallery.*

Floor Plan L

The Yellow Bow Rooms: Servant's Room catalogue

246 **Washstand** with mahogany top, carved and painted in the Chinese style. Original Pavilion furniture, c.1810. (340199)

247 **Pair of Chairs** in beech simulating bamboo, from a set made for various rooms in the Royal Pavilion, probably by Bailey and Sanders, c.1815. Lent by H.M. The Queen.

248 **Argand Lamp** in bronze, with vase-shaped reservoir. Reproduced from an original by Hancock, given by His Grace the Duke of Devonshire in 1991. (341305)

249 **Seven Paintings** in watercolour and bodycolour, scenes of Chinese domestic life. Exported from China to Europe, c.1800. (100844, 103699/704)

The Yellow Bow Room (South) catalogue

250 **Bed** in mahogany, of *lit en bateau* (boat-shaped) form. English, early-nineteenth century, purchased in 1991. The mattresses were hand-made by Heal & Son Ltd. (341289)

251 **Dressing Table** in mahogany with two drawers. English, c.1830. Lent by H.M. The Queen.

252 **Dwarf Wardrobe** in satinwood fitted with drawers in mahogany and two small cupboards above, with ebonised collonettes. Original Pavilion furniture, c.1805. (341295)

253 **Corner Table** in satinwood. Original Pavilion furniture, c.1810. Purchased with assistance of the P.G.F. and the N.A.C.F. in 1977. (330029)

254 **Armchair** in beech, carved and painted to simulate bamboo. Probably made by Elward, Marsh and Tatham for the Pavilion in 1802. Lent by H.M. The Queen.

255 **Four Chairs** in beech simulating bamboo, from a set made for various rooms in the Royal Pavilion, probably by Bailey and Sanders, c.1815. Lent by H.M. The Queen.

256 **Pair of Argand Lamps** in bronze, with vase-shaped reservoir. Reproduced with assistance from the Regency Society of Brighton and Hove in 1994 from an original by Hancock, given by His Grace The Duke of Devonshire in 1991. (341306/7)

257 **Twenty-three Paintings** in watercolour and bodycolour; two series illustrating the production of cotton cloth and processing tea. Exported from China to Europe, c.1800. Purchased in 1984 with the assistance of The Coral Samuel Charitable Trust, the P.G.F. and the Friends. (102721/44)

258 **Pair of Argand Lamps** in brass with matt gilding, urn-shaped reservoirs on circular plinths. Maker unknown, English, c.1820. Purchased in 1992. (341292/3)

259 **Couch** c.1815. Scroll end and detachable side, beechwood legs carved to imitate bamboo. Original Pavilion furniture made by Tatham, Bailey and Sanders. Purchased with the assistance of the P.G.F. in 1995. (341314)

260 **Pair of Specimen Cabinets** in rosewood and lacquer on tall rosewood stands with turned supports. Original Pavilion furniture, c.1805. Lent by H.M. The Queen.

261 **Pair of Secretaires** in mahogany and pine with black and gold lacquer. The upper and lower sections of the front enclose Japanese lacquer panels; the lacquer panels on the sides are, like the remainder. English 1820–30. Lent by H.M. The Queen.

Queen Victoria's Apartments

Floor Plan 

Queen Victoria first visited the Royal Pavilion in 1837. Her initial reaction was cool: 'The Pavilion is a strange, odd, Chinese looking place, both outside and inside. Most of the rooms are low, and I can only see a morsel of the sea, from one of my sitting room windows'. She visited the Pavilion again in 1838 but then did not return until 1842 when her visit coincided with the second anniversary of her marriage to Prince Albert.

The arrangements of the chamber floor had to be adapted for this visit in order to accommodate her husband and two children. Queen Victoria retained her bedroom over the Entrance Hall with the Wardrobe Maid's room to the east and the wardrobe to the north. The Queen's dressers slept above in the four attic rooms. The South Galleries served as breakfast and lunch rooms.

Following the acquisition of the Pavilion by the town of Brighton in 1850 the chamber floor of the Pavilion was converted for use as a civic function and exhibition area. During the 1860s Queen Victoria's bedroom and the adjacent rooms were altered structurally to provide a large single exhibition area. These three rooms, the Queen's bedroom, the Maid's room and the closet have now been restored to reflect as closely as possible the interiors as used by the Queen between 1837 and 1845.

TOP: *Queen Victoria's apartments in use as an exhibition area.*

ABOVE: *The canopy of the bed showing the elaborate draperies based on Thomas King's designs.*

LEFT: *Queen Victoria's bedroom today. The room has been restored to its appearance in the early 1840s.*

BELOW: *The hand-painted wallpaper is a design based on existing fragments.*

Queen Victoria's Bedroom

Originally the room was decorated with a hand-painted Chinese paper, made for the export market. These papers were produced in sets, so that when hung they formed a continuous, unrepeating scene. Using original fragments that have survived and information from other similar sets of papers still in situ in country houses, a set of wallpapers was hand-painted.

The mahogany four-poster bed (furnished with six mattresses of straw, hair and feathers, hand-made by Heal & Son Ltd) was reproduced by courtesy of His Grace The Duke of Wellington from an example at Stratfield Saye in Hampshire. This bed conforms with the description of the bed in Denew's Inventory of the Royal Pavilion which was compiled shortly after Queen Victoria left Brighton. The bed and window curtains in green *gros de nap* (a finely ribbed silk) are based on designs from Thomas King's *The Upholsterer's Guide* of c.1835. The tassels, made of turned wood, covered in alternating silk and wool, derive their shape from originals used elsewhere in the Pavilion. Like other rooms on the Chamber floor these rooms were furnished with a flat-weave Brussels carpet with a pattern of 'drab and flowers'.

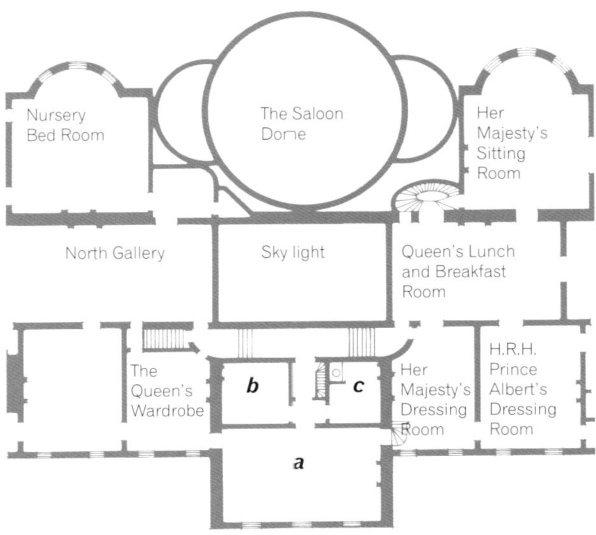

ABOVE: *Plan of the first floor of the Pavilion showing how Queen Victoria used the first floor in the early 1840s. Reproduced by permission of H.M. The Queen.*
The restored apartments are:
a *Queen Victoria's Bedroom*
b *The Maid's Room*
c *The Closet*

RIGHT: *The reproduction four-poster bed furnished with green silk draperies.*

The Maid's Room

The small adjacent room, decorated with a reproduction of the original wallpaper supplied by courtesy of Brunschwig et Fils, has been furnished to recreate the Maid's Room. The 3ft. 6in. tent bedstead has been fitted with a *palliasse* (a straw mattress), a wool mattress and a feather mattress, hand-made by Heal & Son Ltd, with bed hangings in white dimity, a hand-woven ribbed cloth.

The Closet

In George IV's reign this room was used as a servant's room but was subsequently converted into a water closet, either for William IV or Queen Victoria. The design of the panelling is based on a surviving example found in the Yellow Bow Rooms; the bowl and mechanism dates from the second half of the nineteenth century. The wallpaper is a reproduction made and supplied by courtesy of Brunschwig et Fils.

Queen Victoria's Apartments: Bedroom catalogue

The furniture displayed in this room conforms wherever possible with items listed in the inventory made in 1846, following Queen Victoria's last visit to the Pavilion.

262 **Four-poster Bed** in mahogany; reproduced from an original 1830s bed at Stratfield Saye, by courtesy of His Grace The Duke of Wellington. The bed is furnished with draperies in green *gros de nap*, with green silk linings and gold tassels; the design for the bed furnishings and window curtains derives from Thomas King's *The Upholsterer's Guide: Rules for Cutting and forming draperies, valences &c*, first published in the mid 1830s. The six mattresses, filled with straw, hair and feathers, were hand made by Heal & Son Ltd.

263 **Wardrobe** in rosewood veneer on mahogany, with a brass gallery. Original Pavilion furniture. English, c.1800. Purchased with assistance of the P.G.F. in 1963. (340306)

264 **Dressing Table** in rosewood, on turned tapering legs; original Pavilion furniture. English, c.1830. Purchased with assistance from the Friends and the P.G.F. in 1974. (340432)

265 **Mirror** in satinwood. English, c.1790. (340433)

266 **Pillar Table** in rosewood, inlaid with brass with a square top. Original Pavilion furniture. English, c.1815. Purchased with assistance from The Coral Samuel Charitable Trust, the P.G.F. and the Friends in 1979. (340373)

267 **Chair** in beech simulating bamboo, from a set made for various rooms in the Royal Pavilion, probably by Bailey and Sanders, c.1815. (341267)

268 **Arm Chair** in beech, carved and painted to simulate bamboo. Probably made by Elward, Marsh and Tatham for the Pavilion in 1802. Lent by H.M. The Queen.

269 **Argand Lamp** for two lights in brass in Gothic style. English, by Smethurst and Co., London, c.1830. Purchased in 1988. (341275)

270 **Pair of Argand Lamps** in brass, with ovoic reservoirs. English, c.1820. (341287/8)

271 **Argand Lamp** in bronze, with vase-shaped reservoir. Reproduced with assistance from the Regency Society of Brighton and Hove in 1994, from an original by Hancock, given by His Grace the Duke of Devonshire in 1991. (341308)

272 **Workbox** in rosewood with brass inlay. English, c.1820. (340072)

Queen Victoria's Apartments: Maid's Room catalogue

273 **Tent Bed** in mahogany, made by John Durham of 15 Catherine Street, Stand, London, 1823–8. Furnished with dimity hangings (modern); the mattresses in hair and wool were hand made by Heal & Son Ltd. Purchased with assistance of the P.G.F. in 1983. (340321)

274 **Table** in mahogany. Original Pavilion furniture. English, 1790–1800. (340320)

275 **Chair** in beech simulating bamboo, from a set made for various rooms in the Royal Pavilion, probably by Bailey and Sanders, c.1815. (341268)

276 **Argand Lamp** in brass by Smethurst and Co., London, c.1820. (341271)

*On leaving Queen Victoria's apartments visitors pass through a narrow passage to **The South Galleries**.*

The South Galleries

The South Galleries, created during Nash's alterations to the Pavilion, were used as breakfast rooms by the Prince Regent's resident guests. The apartments to the left (east) of the South Galleries were occupied by the Prince himself until infirmity forced him to move to the ground floor; to the right were guest bedrooms.

Lavishly decorated by Frederick Crace, the walls of the South Galleries were painted in vivid azure blue, overlaid with a trellis-work of cut-out strips of paper, block-printed in imitation of bamboo. There were no windows which opened to the exterior (except for one which allowed for 'borrowed' light from the Long Gallery below) but two splendidly decorated laylights. These had painted canvas upstands adorned with dragons and bats on a pale blue background similar in colour to the ceiling and bordered by a richly painted cornice.

The double doors to the bedrooms were finely grained in imitation of pink teawood and flanked by semi-round wooden columns painted with shadowed trellis. The columns stood on simulated marble bases and were topped by crown-like ornaments on which sat kylins (Chinese mythological creatures) carved in wood and richly painted. The flat-weave Brussels carpet with a pattern of 'drab and flowers' is the same as is used elsewhere in the Chamber floor.

ABOVE: The South Galleries *from Nash's* Views.

LEFT: *The South Galleries restored.*

TOP: *Applying blue distemper to the walls.*

ABOVE: *Pasting imitation bamboo strips over the distemper to form the trellis pattern.*

RIGHT : *The South Galleries restored.*

BELOW: *Detail of one of the columns with its painted marble base.*

By the 1930s the South Galleries and the bedrooms to the west had been incorporated into one large function room. As part of the recent structural restoration, the original interior architecture was reinstated and Crace's decorative scheme reproduced. Two of the original columns survived and many of the wooden ornaments (which had been reused throughout the building in subsequent schemes) have been returned to their original location. The principal visual record for the scheme was provided by Pugin's watercolour made for John Nash in 1822.

This, together with the Crace accounts, wallpaper fragments and descriptions in the Royal Pavilion inventory, enabled the interior to be re-created accurately using original methods and materials wherever possible.

The South Galleries catalogue

277 **Sofa** in split cane and bamboo with modern upholstery. Chinese export ware, c.1800. Bought with the assistance of the P.G.F. and the Friends in 1986. (341239)

278 **Six Chairs** in beech simulating bamboo, from a set made for various rooms in the Royal Pavilion, probably by Bailey and Sanders, c.1815. Lent by H.M. The Queen.

279 **Pair of Tables** in bamboo with pine tops, the sides decorated with split bamboo panels. Original Pavilion furniture. Chinese, c.1800. Lent by H.M. The Queen.

280 **Cartel Clock** in ormolu case, with enamel dial, signed 'Chatenay à Versailles'. French, c.1780. Purchased with the assistance of The Coral Samuel Charitable Trust, the P.G.F. and the Friends in 1980. (340317)

281 **Pair of Pagodas** in carved ivory. Chinese, c.1800. Lent by H.M. The Queen.

282 **Pair of Argand Lamps** in bronze, with vase shaped reservoir. Reproduced with assistance from the Regency Society of Brighton and Hove in 1994, from an original by Hancock given by His Grace the Duke of Devonshire in 1991. (341309/10)

283 **Two Stands** in bamboo, hexagonal, with scagliola top and lower platform, one with brass gallery, original Pavilion furniture, c.1800. Lent by H.M. The Queen.

284 **Pair of Garden Seats** in Chinese porcelain. (341312/13)

Visitors now descend the South Staircase, and exit through a section of the servants' passage to the ***Royal Pavilion Shop****.*

On leaving the shop visitors can enjoy a walk around the Royal Pavilion Estate to view not only the restored Pavilion (and related buildings) but also the restored gardens: see pp.74–79 for The Guide to the Royal Pavilion Estate and Gardens.

Living in the Royal Pavilion: Comfort and Convenience

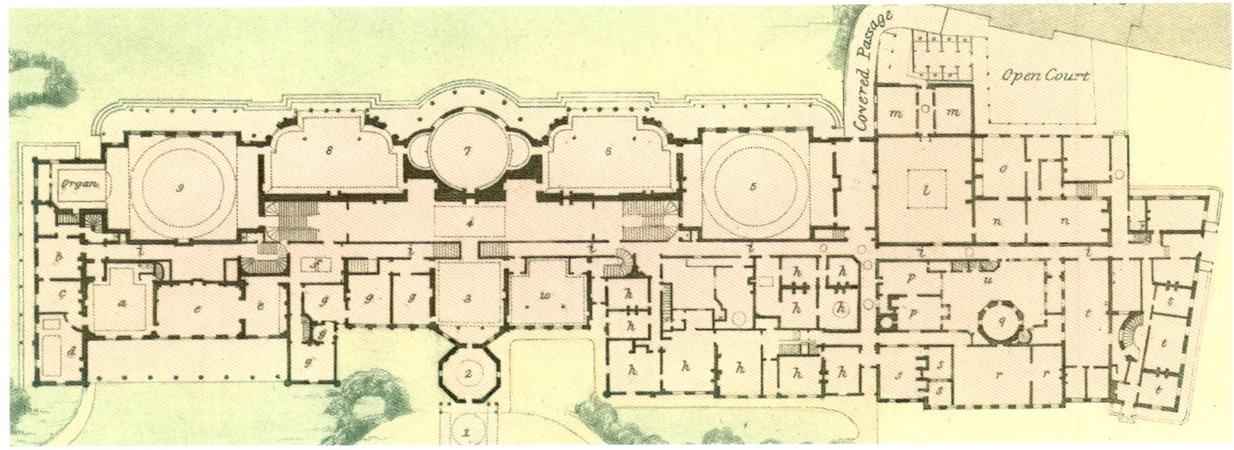

Above: *Ground plan from Nash's* Views *showing the layout of the ground floor during the Royal occupancy. Most of the offices to the south and west of the Great Kitchen were demolished in the second half of the nineteenth century.*

State Apartments

1. Porte Cochère
2. *Octagon Hall*
3. *Entrance Hall*
4. *Long Gallery*
5. *Banqueting Room*
6. *Banqueting Room Gallery*
7. *Saloon*
8. *Music Room Gallery*
9. *Music Room*
10. *Red Drawing Room*

Private Apartments

- a *His Majesty's Bed Room*
- b *Ante Room*
- c *Dressing Room*
- d *Bath*
- e *Libraries*
- f *Ante Room*
- g *Private Secretary's Apartments*
- h *Visitors' Apartments*

Offices

- i *Corridor*
- k *Pages' Room*
- l *King's Kitchen*
- m *Larders*
- n *Kitchen for the Household*
- o *Steaming Kitchen*
- p *Pastry Rooms*
- q *Tower for Water Reservoir*
- r *Pages' Dining Room*
- s *Confectionery*
- t *House Keeper, etc*
- u *Open Court*

For the Prince Regent the Royal Pavilion was a consuming passion that endured for some thirty-five years. He employed not only the most talented architects, artists and craftsmen, but was also determined that the palace should be the ultimate in comfort and convenience. Particular attention was paid by his architect and designers to lighting and heating the interior, as well as providing the most modern equipment for comfort, entertainment and the pursuit of gastronomic pleasures.

The Prince was always particularly concerned to meet the needs and wishes of his guests at the Pavilion. The Comtesse de Boigne noted that on the occasion of her parents' first visit the Prince's butler made enquiries in advance as to the requirements and tastes of his visitors: 'No householder could be more careful than the Prince Regent or more prodigal in small attentions when he wishes to please. No detail was too insignificant for his care'. The small size of the Pavilion limited the number of guests who could stay in the building, and the accomodation that there was would have been reserved for members of the royal family and the royal household. Guests stayed for several days, but rarely for more than a week. They would be joined at dinner by others staying in the town. Dinner in the magnificent Banqueting Room was served at six, followed by conversation, games or musical entertainment, which lasted until the early hours of the morning. Guests had the option of breakfasting in their own rooms or sharing a meal, served on the upper-floor galleries, lit by daylight through the painted skylights. According to the Comtesse de Boigne, certain visitors, such as the Marchioness of Hertford, never appeared publicly for this social occasion 'attempting to hide the irreparable outrages of time'. Nor did the Prince join his guests for breakfast, and for this reason he attached importance to the perfection of this meal; the honours were done by the King's Private Secretary and his wife, Sir Benjamin and Lady Bloomfield.

The Royal Household and the Management of the Royal Pavilion

The Royal Household, which was responsible for the Royal Pavilion, was divided into three large departments, each headed by an Officer of State, who changed with the Government. The Office of Woods and Forests was responsible for the fabric of the building, structural alterations and the exterior including, for example, window cleaning. The Lord Chamberlain's Office was responsible for such matters as interior decorations and refurbishments and the management of some of the servants including the housekeeper, the housemaids and the King's personal staff. The Lord Steward's Office was responsible for the kitchens, the gardens, the supply of foodstuffs, fuel, linen etc. and relevant staff including the Clerk of the Kitchen, cooks and porters.

Absurd situations arose as a result of these divisions of labour; for example the Lord Steward's Office laid a fire, but the Lord Chamberlain's Office was responsible for lighting it. If the heating was inadequate, no single official was accountable or could do anything about it. One department supplied lamps, another cleaned, trimmed and lit them. The resident officer in the palace was the Master of the Household, who belonged to the Lord Steward's department, but had no authority over members of the Lord Chamberlain's Office. In 1844 Baron Stockmar, a close friend of Prince Albert, wrote a memorandum on this confused management and gave the following example of bureaucratic procedures:

> 'If a pane of glass, or the door of a cupboard in the scullery, requires mending, it cannot now be done without the following process: A requisition is prepared and signed by the chief cook, it is then countersigned by the clerk of the kitchen, then it is taken to be signed by the Master of the Household, thence it is taken to the Lord Chamberlain's Office, where it is authorised, and then laid before the Clerk of the Works, under the office of Woods and Forests; and consequently many a window and cupboard have remained broken for months'.

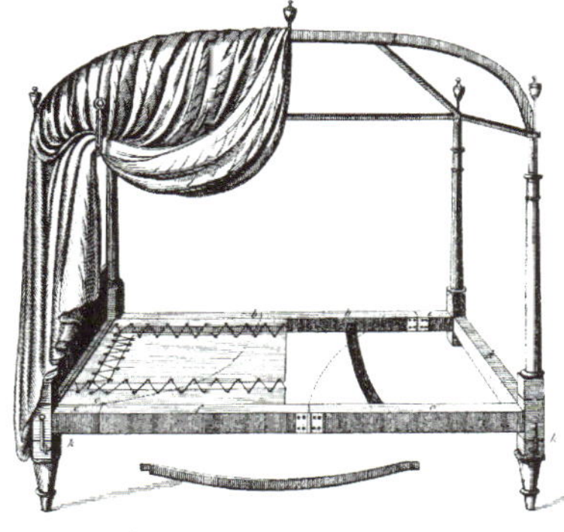

Top: *An illustration from Thomas Sheraton's* The Cabinet Dictionary, *1803, showing a type of bed used in servants' rooms, and how it could be dismantled.*

Above: *Detail from Nash's* Views *showing the King (seated at the centre on the right) entertaining his guests in the Banqueting Room.*

Pay and Conditions

George IV paid his staff quite well by the standards of the day. Members of the Royal Household were paid quarterly; they also received allowances for clothing and lodging. On retirement the pension given to staff was generous and sometimes equivalent to the salary for the post. A list of proposed pensions submitted to the Treasury in 1837 suggested an annual pension of £50 to a housemaid who, after 25 years' service, could no longer undertake her duties owing to ill-health and infirmity.

In 1823 the 'Steward Comptroller of the House Establishment at Brighton' was paid £300 per annum, the housekeeper £112 and ten housemaids £45 10s each. By 1824 Miss Lovatt had been made Housekeeper at the Pavilion and remained in service throughout Queen Victoria's period of residence in Brighton. Accounts for the Lord Chamberlain's department for 1823 recorded the wages of certain members of the Royal Household: Housekeepers (£112–£450 p.a. depending on the royal residence), Housemaids (£45 p.a.), Pages (£30–£290 p.a. depending on rank), Royal Physicians (£214 p.a.), the Royal Apothecary (£229 p.a.), Master of the Music (£262 p.a.), Keeper of the Swans (£28 p.a.), Rat Killer (£80 p.a.), Messengers (£35 p.a.), Gentleman of the Wine Cellar (£37 p.a.) and the Remover of Ashes (£37 p.a.); the Lord Chamberlain and his secretary were the highest paid officials receiving £885 p.a. and £750 p.a. respectively.

Accomodation

Most servants arrived with the King at the start of his winter visits, though a small group of domestic staff maintained the building throughout the year. Appropriate members of the Royal Household, and friends and advisers, accompanied the King on his visits to Brighton. The King's Private Secretary occupied rooms above the King's private apartments in the Royal Pavilion; the Lord Steward had his own separate apartments in 'Shergold's House', a building adjacent to the Pavilion on the Steine.

The quality of accommodation allocated to different members of the Royal Household depended obviously on their rank and the space available. The very small room for a servant adjoining the Duke of York's bedroom was fitted with a high mahogany press bedstead 6ft. 9in. high by 3ft. wide; with the additional pieces of furniture listed in the Pavilion's inventory (a chest of drawers, a dressing glass, a corner wash-hand stand, a table and two chairs) there can have been very little room when the fold-up or press bed was in use. More spacious servants' rooms in the Pavilion were equipped with a tent bedstead with dimity (a woven ribbed cloth) furnishings, similar in design to the bed now displayed in the Maid's Room in Queen Victoria's Apartments. The bed was supplied with a straw *palliasse*, one hair and one feather mattress, a bolster, pillows and three blankets. Other furniture usually included a chest of drawers, a dressing glass, a wash-hand stand and some chairs.

Above: *Detail from Nash's* Views *illustrating on the far right the octagonal water tower which supplied the Pavilion with water. Nash designed the tower to add to the picturesque effect of the roofline.*

Below: *Detail from Nash's* Views *showing the steam table which enabled prepared dishes to be kept warm before being taken through to the Banqueting Room.*

The Kitchens

The preparation and consumption of food were key activities in the social life of the Pavilion. As can be seen from the ground plan, a large proportion of the space available was allocated by Nash to the Great Kitchen and the range of ancillary kitchens and offices located to the south and west, around the water tower. The tower, in an open courtyard, pumped well-water to a large lead tank, which, through an iron mains and extensive pipe system, serviced all parts of the Pavilion. Unfortunately, all the kitchens and courtyard area south of the Great Kitchen were demolished in the late nineteenth century.

Five rooms, devoted to the preparation of confectionery and pastries, were equipped with stewing stoves, ovens and hot closets. Ice was stored in lead ice-bins in the ice room, adjacent to the Confectioner's Room, in which elaborate confections, sorbets and creams were prepared.

The household (or 'family') kitchen and scullery serviced the royal household and were probably used for preparing meals for the Prince on private occasions. Two larders were located east of the Great Kitchen. They were equipped with square iron frames, fixed to the ceiling and fitted with tinned-iron meat hooks; lined troughs were supplied to catch the drips from the game. The bakehouse, near the larders, was equipped with bread furnace-ovens and a 6ft kneading trough; a large steam room with steam boilers was next to the Great Kitchen. Other rooms were used for storage and for cleaning plate.

The Great Kitchen itself, illustrated in Nash's *Views of the Royal Pavilion* (1826), was a source of wonder to contemporary observers: C. Wright, in *The Brighton Ambulator* (1818), remarked that 'in the furnishing of the kitchen and other offices every modern improvement to facilitate the process of the culinary art has been introduced in all its boasted perfection. It is not exceeding the faithful observation of a narrator, in stating that the recency of the above alterations forms one part of the most useful and convenient appendages to a mansion that is to be seen in the British Empire.'

The aquatint of the kitchen in Nash's *Views* vividly portrays the activities of the Great Kitchen: a chef directs his staff, who are chopping, preparing meats and sauces and stoking the fire for the spit; a footman carries a tray of prepared dishes towards the west door. In the centre, flanked by four large, L-shaped beech preparation tables, is a 13ft.-long oval table, which was praised by Wright: 'With its multiplicity of conducting pipes to throw on and carry off the waste water, [it] is an admirable specimen of mechanical inventions.'

The steam table, installed by William Stark in 1817, was fitted with a cast-iron top, and bound in brass. Food, prepared and arranged on silver dishes, was kept warm on the table, which was covered with a cloth. It was supplied with steam from 'a very large strong copper steam boiler' located behind the kitchen range; cisterns were provided to receive the condensed water, to be conveyed to the drains. This allowed numerous prepared dishes to be kept warm ready to be served in the Banqueting Room, located conveniently close to the kitchens. The table, like the steam kettles and hot closets, was heated by the main and scullery boilers by means of an extensive copper piping system.

No expense was spared in furnishing the kitchen areas: two bills from Stark for the supply and installation of equipment in 1817–18 exceed £6,000. In addition to the items already mentioned, he supplied the copper tent-like awnings, fitted with gutters to receive drips of condensation. These canopies were placed over the stewing and broiling stoves, ovens and kitchen range on the north and south walls to draw away excess heat, smells and steam.

No restraint was shown by the Prince Regent in equipping the culinary offices in the pursuit of haute cuisine, nor in attempting to lure the greatest chefs of the day to prepare banquets for his guests. In 1817 the renowned French chef Marie-Antoine Carême (1784–1833) prepared an elaborate banquet which included thirty-six entrées. No financial remuneration, however, was sufficient to tempt Carême to leave his native country and join the Prince's service.

ABOVE: A Voluptuary under the Horrors of Digestion, *by J. Gillray, caricaturing George's love of food and drink.*

The Ice House

The ice house that had served the Pavilion since the 1790s stood in the south-west corner of the grounds, near to New Road (see plan of the Royal Pavilion Estate, p.74). Ice was brought to the ice room in the Pavilion, which was adjacent to the Confectioner's room where elaborate sorbets and confections were prepared.

In cold winters ice was collected in carts from local ponds, ditches, rivers and streams. Alternatively it could be imported from Norway or North America. A notice in the *Brighton Gazette* in January 1827 records that local confectioners collected ice and deposited it in the Pavilion's ice house.

Ice houses with a pit or well were prepared by placing layers of straw on floors and walls to provide better insulation. Good drainage was essential, and a chalk-soil location was ideal. In proper conditions ice would last all summer, providing a continuous supply for culinary and medical uses. Ice houses could also be used as larders to preserve game, fish, poultry, butter, etc. during the heat of the summer.

Above: *Detail of* The Octagon Hall *from Nash's* Views, *showing the brass stove, the patterned oil cloth and hearth rugs. An Argand lamp, which could be used by footmen to guide arriving guests at night, sits on the chimney-piece.*

Below: *Detail of* The Saloon *from Nash's* Views *showing the luxurious hand-knotted Axminster carpet.*

Heating Systems

On visiting the Pavilion, The Dowager Countess of Ilchester recalled how she was charmed by the gay Chinese scene and the relaxed cordial atmosphere, but commented on the extreme warmth that pervaded the interior, as did many other visitors.

During the Regency period the Pavilion was heated by open fires and an under-floor hot-air heating system. Accounts for 1821 record the installation of a powerful hot-air stove, with flues and cold-air drains in the North End basement. Later that year the floors in the Saloon, Music Room and Banqueting Room Galleries were taken up and made good following the installation of hot-air flues. It would seem that the eastern suite of rooms were all heated by an under-floor hot-air system, supplied from stoves in the basement.

Queen Victoria found the heating and ventilation of the Pavilion unsatisfactory. Even today the temperature in the Pavilion ranges from extreme cold in winter (as current systems are inadequate to heat the high-ceilinged rooms) to hot and stuffy in the summer as the glass laylights convert the atmosphere on the first floor to one of a conservatory. Following the Queen's visit in the spring of 1842, Dr David Boswell Reid (1805–63), renowned for his works at the Houses of Parliament, was called upon to provide proposals for improving the heating and ventilation of the Pavilion. Reid commented in his report that

> '… though the arrangements at the Pavilion may have been attended with considerable expense, the extreme peculiarity of structure, and the total absence of an adequate supply of air, rendered it impossible to attempt any amelioration of the state of the atmosphere in the apartments to which my attention was directed without considerable alterations.'

The installation of ventilation shafts in the Pavilion's unusual and complex structure proved difficult and specification of his heating and ventilation system is unknown. Existing fireplaces in certain areas such as the Long Gallery were replaced with hot-air stoves and the chimneys were altered; new hot-air stoves were installed, for example, in the small room under the south staircase, in the kitchen areas and in the basement.

Carpets and Floor Coverings

The treatment of the floors in the Royal Pavilion reflected the function and social grandeur of individual rooms. The main State Rooms – the Music Room, Saloon and Banqueting Room – were fitted with luxurious hand-knotted cut-pile Axminster carpets of elaborate design and 'planned to the room' (i.e. wall-to-wall). Areas subject to very heavy wear and dirt such as the Octagon Hall, the Deckers' Room and the passage behind the King's Apartments were covered with oil cloth, a type of hard-wearing painted canvas. These could be plain in colour or patterned: the Octagon Hall was

furnished with 'a matt pattern buff oil cloth'; the Servants' Passage behind the King's Apartments with a 'drab rosette and mottled ground' cloth. Other areas subject to hard wear were covered with drugget, a felted wool cloth similar to felt: the Entrance Hall had grey drugget with a crimson and black border planned to the room. The panels of the treads of the north and south cast-iron staircases were also fitted with grey and crimson drugget.

Other rooms such as the Long Gallery, the Music Room and Banqueting Room Galleries on the ground floor and the bedrooms and Galleries on the first floor were fitted with Brussels carpet, an uncut loop-pile carpet, usually manufactured in widths of 27in. It was a relatively cheap and durable form of carpeting, easy to lay wall-to-wall as it was made in narrow strips. The Brussels carpets were patterned, as for example the carpet in the South Galleries, which was described in the inventory as 'a drab ground flowered Brussels carpet'. Most rooms were also furnished with hearth rugs.

In contrast to the repeat patterned woven Brussels carpeting in adjacent rooms, the hand-knotted Axminster carpets made for the main State Rooms allowed more flexibility in design and colouring. Fitted wall-to-wall, each carpet drew together the decorative elements of the rooms with an elaborate overall design. The Banqueting Room carpet reflected the design of the magnificent central chandelier with a dragon and lotus centre in a coloured sunflower against a blue ground.

All the public rooms in the Pavilion were fitted with wall-to-wall carpeting. When social occasions required areas for dancing, carpets were removed and floors chalked with decorative patterns to create a suitable surface.

Above: *Detail of* The Long Gallery *from Nash's* Views *showing the fitted Brussels carpet. Brussels carpet was relatively cheap and ideally suited for areas that received considerable wear.*

Bathroom Facilities

Sadly, the King's bathroom, which was adjacent to his bedroom with access through a jib door, was removed in the nineteenth century. The 1820s inventory, however, records the extensive equipment installed for the King's pleasure: 'a plunging bath lined with veined marble 16ft by 10ft … 8 veined marble steps', 'a vapour bath in a mahogany frame', 'a large warm bath with mahogany panelled case and cover', 'a shower bath' and 'a douche bath'.

The plunge bath was supplied with fresh as well as salt water pumped from the sea to a tank which was located in the garden and served as a reservoir. A boiler was fitted which supplied hot salt water for therapeutic baths for the King.

The King's guests, by contrast, were supplied with portable metal hip baths as required; most bedrooms were provided with plumbed-in water closets.

Water Closets

The water closets throughout the Pavilion were supplied with water from cisterns. On the first floor these were located in the roof above the bedrooms. Water was pumped throughout the building through iron mains and lead pipes by a forcing engine in the Water Tower, which was located in the kitchen courtyard to the south. The closets were regularly cleaned and the moving parts oiled. Generally the seats were made of mahogany and the backs panelled in cedar to conceal the pipes and mechanism.

Most bedrooms in the Pavilion were furnished with 'a night convenience' or a chamber pot, sometimes placed in a bedside 'pedestal' or cabinet. His Majesty's bedroom was furnished with a mahogany night convenience, a water closet with a mahogany seat and cedar back and a bidet chair. The bidet chair, designed to the bamboo pattern of other furniture in the Pavilion, concealed a tin or earthenware pan; the back and seat cover were caned and the edge of the seat stuffed and covered with blue leather.

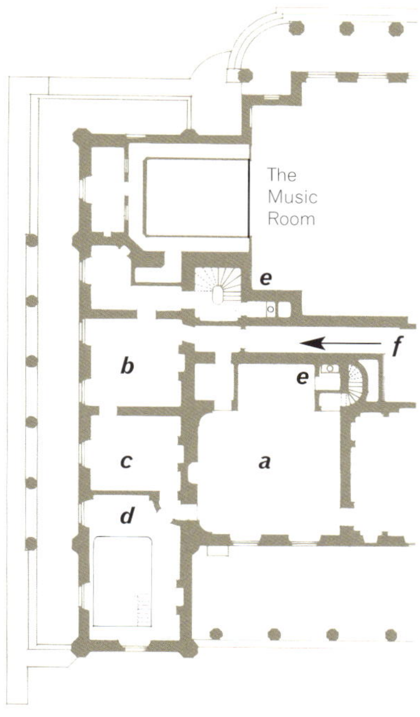

Above: *Detail of ground plan showing the location of the bathroom in the King's Private Apartments.*

- **a** *His Majesty's Bedroom*
- **b** *Wardrobe*
- **c** *Page's Room*
- **d** *Bath; the location of the large plunge bath is indicated on the plan*
- **e** *Water closet and Servants' staircase*
- **f** *Servants' corridor*

TOP: *Frederick Crace's design for a Chinese lantern. Similar lanterns were used in the early chinoiserie schemes throughout the Pavilion.*

ABOVE: *One of the eight original lamps from the Banqueting Room, designed by Robert Jones. The lamps were subsequently converted for gas and later electricity.*

Lighting

For some contemporary observers the over-heated interior of the Royal Pavilion was excessively opulent and theatrical, and the design and rich decorations too grand for its size and provincial location. Lighting played a key role in the overall effect: 'the lights are dazzling' noted Princess Lieven in 1822, whilst also commenting on the luxurious and 'effeminate' atmosphere of the Pavilion. Lighting by day (as well as by night) was crucial in creating the dramatic atmosphere of the Pavilion's elaborate interiors.

The form of lighting was determined by the size, location and function of the different rooms, providing in each area a particular and individual atmosphere. Nash introduced dramatic light sources from above to illuminate both the chamber and ground floors. The Long Gallery, for example, was lit by day by three tall windows of painted glass at each end, and a large central painted skylight (flanked by two vertical painted windows) which pierced the first floor to allow muted natural light to illuminate the central area of the Gallery, where visitors entered. All the galleries and stairwells on the chamber floor were also lit by large painted skylights. The main rooms on the east front (Saloon, Music and Banqueting Rooms) had full-length arched French windows; the two latter rooms were also illuminated by elliptical painted glass windows at clerestory level. The overall effect created was of a colourful, light interior, reminiscent of a garden pavilion, and full of sunlight softened by the hues of the painted glass.

The designs of the chandeliers in the major rooms are integral to each scheme, and form dramatic decorative features. Perhaps the most flamboyant is the chandelier in the Banqueting Room, 30ft. high and weighing nearly a ton, designed by Robert Jones. Hovering in the apex of the domed ceiling is a carved and silvered dragon, holding in its claws the lustre of cascades of glass, flanked by six carved wooden dragons, their heads arched as if to exhale light 'each bearing a large painted ground glass lotus for a lamp with burners'. The size and weight of this chandelier is said to have frightened Queen Adelaide who feared it might fall on the assembled company. In 1833 it was removed to store by William IV, where it remained until Queen Victoria reinstated it in 1842.

At night the interior of the Pavilion was lit by a combination of candles, oil lamps and gas. Lighting the chandeliers must have been a considerable task for the lamp-lighters, who were supplied with robustly built pairs of very high steps with platforms for use in the Banqueting Room. Each room was furnished with appropriately designed chandeliers, lanterns, oil table lamps, torchères or candelabra to such a degree that James Wilson Croker, a frequent visitor, was moved to describe the Pavilion as being 'as full of lamps as Hancock's shop'.

The Lamp Room, located at the south end near the kitchen and household offices, was fitted with floor-to-ceiling closets and presses, a dresser, shelves and a lead sink. Lamp stools, with carpeted tops, and mahogany lamp steps were stored here for use by the lamp-lighters. The inventory of 1828 records the contents of the Oil Cellar: '9 large oil vats with their brass cocks, 2 tin oil pumps and 5 large oil cans, 26 gallon tin measures, 2 one gallon ditto and 2 funnels'. Another lamp room was located in the north end basement, used as a store and for trimming lamps.

The smoke from the numerous chandeliers, lanterns and oil lamps that lit the interior so brilliantly inevitably caused damage to the paint-work and ceilings, necessitating regular cleaning. The Crace accounts include bills for the Saloon for 'cleaning and repairing the whole of the ornamental painting, being very much injured by smoke of lamps' and for cleaning paintwork and skylights in the Long Gallery, 'much damaged by the smoke of lanthorns'.

Gas was little used in England to light interiors in the first decades of the nineteenth century. The way in which gas lighting was used in the

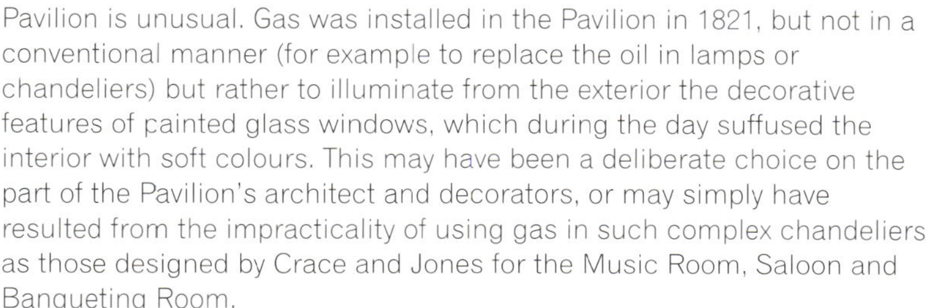

Pavilion is unusual. Gas was installed in the Pavilion in 1821, but not in a conventional manner (for example to replace the oil in lamps or chandeliers) but rather to illuminate from the exterior the decorative features of painted glass windows, which during the day suffused the interior with soft colours. This may have been a deliberate choice on the part of the Pavilion's architect and decorators, or may simply have resulted from the impracticality of using gas in such complex chandeliers as those designed by Crace and Jones for the Music Room, Saloon and Banqueting Room.

For over a century publications have so frequently recorded that George IV had the Music Room and Banqueting Room lit by gas that the term 'gasolier' has crept into recent literature on the the chandeliers in the Music Room. It would seem from contemporary information that, in fact, these rooms were only lit by gas from the exterior, at high levels, and that the chandeliers themselves were lit with oil lamps or candles.

At night the painted elliptical windows at clerestory level in the Music Room and Banqueting Room were illuminated from the exterior, thus casting some light on the richly decorated ceilings. It seems that the sets of painted glass windows above the bamboo staircases were also back-lit at night illuminating the stair wells and galleries with soft tones.

After the town of Brighton acquired the Royal Pavilion in 1850 the use of gas lighting was extended to all the pendant lights in the main State Rooms, the King's Apartments and the Corridor and some first floor rooms. The Pavilion followed closely on the pioneers of electric lighting, and was partially converted to electricity in 1883 under the direction of Magnus Volk, a local electrical engineer and the creator of Volk's Electric Railway.

TOP RIGHT: *Part of the central chandelier in the Banqueting Room. The dragons throw their heads backwards as if exhaling light through the glass shades.*

ABOVE: *Detail of* The King's Bedroom *from Nash's* Views *showing the oil lamps made of 'Japan Jars' with metal stems and ground glass lotus shades.*

TOP LEFT: *Detail of the cross-section of* The Music Room *from Nash's* Views. *The high-level elliptical windows above the curtains were lit at night from outside by gas.*

The Restoration of the Royal Pavilion: Structure, Interior and Gardens

ABOVE: *The Pavilion shrouded in scaffolding.*

The Restoration of the Structure, 1980–1992

As it stands today, the Pavilion is largely the creation of John Nash who superimposed a fantasy of oriental domes and minarets upon the earlier classical villa of Henry Holland. However, this remodelling which gave rise to the exotic splendour of the Pavilion, introduced a variety of structural problems which subsequently threatened the very survival of the building. In the early 1980s a major restoration programme commenced to restore both the structure of the building and the elaborate carved stonework.

Water penetration

The Royal Pavilion began to leak soon after it was completed. Building accounts for the late 1820s include references to works required following outbreaks of dry rot caused by water penetration. Major causes were the complex structure of the roofs and Nash's idiosyncratic construction techniques. Nash's cupolas were covered with mastic on iron sheeting nailed to timber cladding. This ingenious method may have been a perfect solution in an ideal atmosphere, but in the wet British climate, the render cracked and water seeped through to rust the iron and rot the timbers.

In enlarging and extending Holland's original building, Nash was also faced with the prospect of a considerably increased volume of rainwater to disperse at roof level. Former outlets and external down-pipes became internal, marooned by increasingly large roof areas, which also resulted in the formation of valley gutters between pitches.

To avoid visual disfigurement of the new oriental facades, rainwater pipes were generally concealed by building them into the structure, and increased volumes of water were channelled into inadequate internal pipes. These internal drains inevitably became blocked; water overflowed and penetrated the fabric of the building. This promoted wet and dry rot, beetle infestation in timbers and corrosion of the iron framing structure. Rainwater down-pipes had to be renewed and enlarged, and new materials enabled jointless lengths of pipework to be introduced in inaccessible 'built-in' locations.

The restoration programme provided the opportunity to reinstate the original Nash roof line by the removal of later alterations which had heightened the first floor rooms at the south end of the building. This resulted in the re-creation of the South Galleries, reopened in 1992, (see pp.55–57).

Wet and dry rot

With the Pavilion's high proportion of structural timber elements and the continued ingress of moisture, rampant dry rot was the inevitable consequence. At one period, the roofs of both the Music and Banqueting Rooms were in danger of collapsing through the ceilings below owing to the rotting of the laminated beam ends which supported the characteristic tented roofs.

The traditional method of dealing with dry rot is to cut out and completely remove the affected timbers and replace them with new wood. In the case of the Pavilion, this was often impossible because of the unique original interior finishes supported by the affected timbers. Therefore, a process of preservation by remission was employed. This entailed reinforcing the affected timber, the removal of conditions promoting the rot (for example the prevention of further moisture penetration) and the introduction of ventilation. Continued monitoring of environmental conditions is crucial to ensure that known locations of rot are not reactivated. A comprehensive inspection programme is in place, assisted by a computer data-logging system which monitors several hundred moisture sensors in inaccessible areas and water level sensors in twenty-five sumps.

Stonework

The adventurous structural use of iron within stone features enabled Nash to effect the transition from Holland's classical Pavilion to the Pavilion as we know it today: minarets are supported by iron cores, and stone sections were frequently connected by clamps or iron framing.

Moisture penetration led to the iron cores rusting and expanding, which cracked the stone and allowed further water penetration. Added to this was damage caused by the salty atmosphere and traffic pollution. By the mid-twentieth century it was clear that the stonework was in serious need of restoration, repair and replacement.

In the late 1960s, ten of the minarets were judged unsafe and removed and replaced with fibre-glass replicas; in 1980 a detailed survey revealed the true extent of the stone repairs urgently needed. This survey was instrumental in initiating the structural restoration, and throughout the following twelve-year programme the principle was established, whenever possible, to replace materials with similar 'authentic' materials.

In some cases it was not easy to establish the original design from decayed or severely damaged stone decoration. The restoration of the Pavilion to its original appearance proved problematic owing to the paucity of contemporary information available. Although a number of watercolours by Pugin left a detailed record of the early appearance of the building, architectural records were limited to some mid-nineteenth century plans and a few drawings. In the absence of any of Nash's original working drawings, old visual records and knowledge derived from earlier restoration works proved vital.

All the 1960s fibre-glass minarets have now been replaced with Bath stone and all the severely corroded and dangerous stonework has been replaced. The minarets at the north end of the building are mostly original, having been sensitively restored.

With the completion of the structural restoration, the building emerged from a chrysalis of the largest self-supporting scaffold span and protective blue sheeting ever erected in this country. Following the restoration of the stonework and roofs the rendered parts of the building were painted in the original stone colour to re-create Nash's picturesque vision of a delicate Indian palace built of stone. To enhance this effect the external render was lined out to create an illusion of blocks of stone, a technique used by Nash in the 1820s.

ABOVE: *An example of stonework badly corroded by water penetration.*

BELOW: *The Saloon with the floor boards removed following the discovery of dry rot and insect infestation.*

RIGHT: The Music Room, *by A. Penley, 1851, showing the Grand Ball which took place in January 1851 to mark the reopening of the Pavilion after the redecoration of the ground floor rooms by Wren Vick.*

BOTTOM LEFT: *The Banqueting Room, c.1866. In this scheme, Dury was able to incorporate some of the original canvases returned by Queen Victoria.*

BOTTOM RIGHT: Design for the Banqueting Room Gallery, *by J. D. Crace, 1898. In this highly decorative Moorish design no attempt was made by Crace at restoration or reinterpretation of the original scheme. Reproduced by courtesy of the Board of Trustees of the Victoria & Albert Museum.*

The Restoration of the Interior

The Nineteenth Century

The problems encountered today in restoring the interior of the Royal Pavilion date from the late 1840s when Queen Victoria decided to sell the Pavilion and acquired a new residence, Osborne House, on the Isle of Wight. Before the Pavilion was purchased by the town of Brighton in 1850 its magnificent rooms had been completely stripped and left in a dilapidated state: 'Scarcely more than the bare walls remained, for the chimney-pieces had been torn down; the chandeliers, the organ, and even the grates removed; the Music Room stripped of its beautiful Chinese paintings, and the whole place dismantled and disfigured, as though its doom had been fixed'. (see Aldrich p.167)

Once the Pavilion became the responsibility of Brighton, a Committee was established to oversee the complete refurbishment of the interior. Within a year the ground floor had been redecorated by Christopher Wren Vick, a Brighton-based decorator who had worked for both William IV and Queen Victoria. His sympathetic scheme, for the most part based on the original Regency decorations that he had known well, also included the installation of Caen stone chimney-pieces designed by John Thomas. Some of these, for example in the Banqueting Room, still remain *in situ* today.

A second phase of redecoration was brought about partly by the return of original wall paintings and fittings by Queen Victoria in 1864 and partly by the then shabby state of decoration of the ground floor rooms. An expatriate French artist, Antoine Dury, undertook this project incorporating original features where possible: the original Music Room canvases and chandeliers were reinstated as well as some canvases and the magnificent dragon chandelier in the Banqueting Room. To complete the decorative scheme in the Banqueting Room, Dury painted new canvases in Chinese style in sympathy with Robert Jones' originals. These remain an integral part of the Banqueting Room decorations today.

Further works were undertaken in the 1880s and 1890s by John Dibblee Crace (1838–1919), the grandson of Frederick Crace (1779–1859) who had designed much of the original decoration.

In particular the North and South Drawing Rooms (as the Music Room and Banqueting Room Galleries were named in the Victorian period) were redecorated. Although nearly all the wall coverings, furniture and fixtures had been stripped by Queen Victoria, the magnificent ceilings in the Music Room, Saloon and Banqueting Room remained intact. This seems to have determined a policy in the late-nineteenth century of restoring (as then conceived) these rooms to their Regency appearance, but completely redecorating other rooms which retained no original elements. The South Drawing Room, for example, was lavishly decorated by J. D. Crace in Moorish style with a heavy embossed linen paper with a design of Moorish arches in bronze against a dull red background surmounted by a frieze in gold and blue. No attempt was made at restoration; these schemes were highly praised by contemporaries as exemplifying 'the finest specimens of decorative Art in Brighton'.

Further original elements from the Pavilion were returned to Brighton by Queen Victoria in the 1890s and incorporated into restorations of various rooms. Following extensive works to the Music Room, J. D. Crace undertook his last major project in Brighton in the spring of 1899 – the restoration of the Banqueting Room. In his report to the Committee following his inspection of the interior he assumes that the intention is to 'retain its original features by restoring the more artistic portions of the work and cleaning and renovating what is in a condition to be preserved with advantage'. He recommended considerable repainting, notably of the sky ceiling and palm leaves, glass, the wall paintings and the pendentives, and the regilding of much carved ornament. The room underwent further 'improvements' with the installation of radiators, a new oak floor, and curtains.

Historians this century have generally denigrated the Victorian phase of the Pavilion's history; undoubtedly by today's standards Victorian restoration works tended to be crude and insensitive, involving much over-painting. In the 1890s, however, they were much admired by contemporaries and as a result civic pride in the Royal Pavilion was maintained, so ensuring its future.

The Twentieth Century

During the First World War, when the building was used as a hospital for Indian soldiers, the interiors were altered, damaged and inevitably neglected. In 1920 when Henry Roberts was made director, a programme of restoration began, funded by a settlement made by the government for the damage done to the building during the war. Attempts were made for the first time to reveal the brilliant colours of the original interiors by removing the layers of overpaint and discoloured varnish applied by the Victorian decorators. Although there was little opportunity to furnish the rooms (which were still used primarily for functions), wherever possible they were conscientiously restored. The murals in both the Music Room and the Banqueting Room were cleaned, as were the existing decorations in the corridor.

Impetus for the work of refurbishment was given by the interest of Queen Mary in the Pavilion. She visited the building on many occasions and returned original items that had remained unused in store at Buckingham Palace. In 1920 she returned the original eight Spode china and ormolu lampstands to the Banqueting Room. These were the first free-standing pieces to come back to the Pavilion. In the 1930s the pilaster ornaments from the Saloon were returned. These were reinstated, along with the original doors and some Chinese papers which, given by Queen Victoria, had been in store in the Pavilion since the nineteenth century.

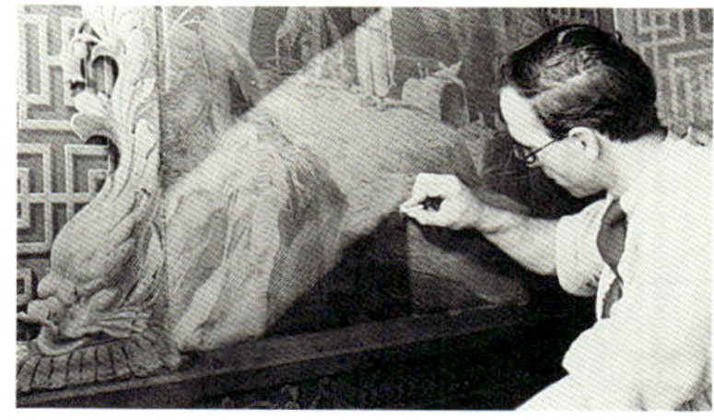

ABOVE: *Roy Bradley cleaning the Music Room murals in c.1949.*

The restoration of the pelmet dragons following the fire of 1975.

FROM TOP TO BOTTOM:

A dragon severely damaged by fire.

Restoration in progress in the workshop.

Applying gesso prior to gilding.

A restored gilt dragon returned to its original position in the Music Room.

ABOVE: *A fire-damaged dragon from the central chandelier in the Music Room being re-gilded.*

BOTTOM LEFT: *The restored dragon returned to the central chandelier in the Music Room.*

BOTTOM RIGHT: *Detail of the completed mirror frame, in situ in the Music Room.*

Roberts was the first director to examine original archives and accounts in order to establish how the Pavilion must have appeared originally. By an extraordinary coincidence an important set of accounts came to light during the 1930s. In 1932, Lady Gordon Lennox visited the Pavilion. She was inspired by the decorations in the corridor and determined to hand paint the design on silk to make curtains. She bought the silk from a firm called Cowtan and Sons, who, it transpired, had taken over the business and accounts of the Crace family in 1899. Mr Cowtan gave the Royal Pavilion a transcript of accounts relating to the Pavilion and the details contained in these accounts have subsequently proved invaluable to the work of restoration. The typewritten transcript is now all that remains of the many volumes of accounts relating to the Crace business, as the original records were destroyed during the London Blitz.

The Second World War caused another break in the progress of restoration, but the work recommenced in 1945 under the direction of Clifford Musgrave. The 1930s and 1940s were marked by a revival of interest in the Regency period. The Regency Society of Brighton and Hove was formed in 1945. The following year saw the State Rooms of the Pavilion adorned with appropriate furniture for the first time for almost 100 years for the first Regency Exhibition. Under the patronage of Queen Mary, this display included loans of original material from the Royal Collections. These annual summer exhibitions continued until the late 1970s, when a policy of furnishing the main State Rooms all year round was introduced.

These exhibitions coincided with the programme of internal restoration, begun in 1945, and the appointment of the first artist-restorer, Roy Bradley. Not only were discoloured layers of varnish removed from painted surfaces, but attempts were now made to re-create some of the interiors lost following alterations to the fabric during the Victorian period. These changes had disrupted the understanding of the Pavilion as the artistic whole created by George IV and his designers. Bradley worked with Musgrave and subsequent directors, making use of every piece of evidence available – original sketches, drawings and prints, archives and accounts, and paint scrapes – to ensure that the work of re-creation was as accurate as possible. The King's Apartments, for example, were decorated with a hand-painted facsimile of the green 'dragon' paper which had once hung there.

Once again the generosity of the Royal Family helped in the realisation of these projects. In the mid 1950s Queen Elizabeth II returned, on loan, a substantial collection, including original items from the Long Gallery, which by then had been restored to its original Crace scheme.

Sadly, however, the programme of restoration and refurbishment was halted in 1975 when the Music Room was badly damaged by an arson attack. Although all but one of the murals escaped serious damage, the decoration above the level of the coving was badly burnt. The room was virtually closed to the public for eleven years while the damage was

repaired, funded by an insurance settlement. A trained conservation team was established to undertake the considerable task of restoring the many damaged ornaments. It took seven people seven months to re-gild the 26,000 cockle shells of the dome; the chandeliers and coving were restored, and replica curtains and a carpet, based on original fragments and archive documentation, were installed.

While investigating the level of damage within the room it was found that the roof itself was dangerously weakened by dry rot, and a massive programme of structural restoration began, which finished in 1992. Meanwhile, just as the Music Room was nearing completion, it was overtaken by another disaster; in the great storm of 1987 a ball of stone was dislodged from a minaret, fell through the newly restored cove, and buried itself in the floor. Restoration work commenced again. At the same time, a replica of the original mirror frame (now in Buckingham Palace) was carved and gilded by the conservation team. It took approximately 187 days to carve the four columns of the frame, which, amongst other details, has some 796 gilded flowers.

Since the completion of the Music Room, work has been concentrated on the first floor of the Pavilion, with the aim of increasing the visitors' understanding of how the Pavilion was used both in George IV's and Queen Victoria's day. The reinstatement of the original interior architecture (part of the structural-restoration programme) made possible the restoration of Queen Victoria's Apartments, the South Galleries and the Yellow Bow Rooms. Items original to the Pavilion that had been in store for 150 years were cleaned and repaired; missing decorations and soft furnishings have been re-created based on historical evidence and using traditional materials and techniques wherever possible. On the first floor a fine set of Chinese wallpapers, still in its original setting in the Adelaide Corridor, was restored and protected with new showcases.

Since 1975 resources have been devoted to these major projects. As a result some other areas in the Pavilion are in need of conservation treatment; hundreds of thousands of visitors per year inflict considerable wear and tear on the building. In future the conservation programme will be divided between caring for the existing fabric of the building by a careful schedule of cleaning and conservation, together with other projects involving the re-creation of 'lost features', which help to bring the building alive for visitors. One such project was the making of a replica of the 'Rock Clock' for the Music Room (the original is in Buckingham Palace) sponsored by the Regency Society of Brighton and Hove, who have always generously supported restoration projects in the Royal Pavilion.

Looking back at the history of the restoration within the Pavilion one sees a succession of gifted visionaries and generous individuals, who, by their enthusiasm, have been able to keep the Pavilion in the public eye, saving it from demolition on more than one occasion. Now its place will be secured into the next century and thereafter.

From top to bottom:

Hanging the dado in the Yellow Bow Rooms.

Surface cleaning the Chinese wallpaper in the Saloon.

Removing the layers of later varnish from one of the kylins from the South Galleries to reveal the original colours.

One of the new glass clerestory panels for the Entrance Hall being painted to recreate Crace's original design.

Bottom left: *The hand-knotted Music Room carpet was made specially for the Pavilion at Killybegs, Ireland.*

Bottom right: *The stone ball, dislodged during the storm of 1987 embedded in the Music Room carpet.*

Above: *Until recently a tarmac road separated the west front of the Pavilion from the gardens.*

Below: The West Front *from Nash's* Views *showing the original picturesque planting scheme on which the restoration of the garden is based.*

The Restoration of the Gardens

John Nash's design for the gardens and grounds of the Royal Pavilion reflects the great revolution in landscape gardening that began in the 1730s. The previously fashionable formality of French-inspired gardens was banished, to be replaced with more natural groupings of trees and shrubs and the creation of picturesque views.

The aquatints of the exterior of the Pavilion in John Nash's *Views* of 1826 give an idea of these principles put into practice with shrubs and thickets gracefully undulating over the lawns. Nash's elegant design had, however, gradually been destroyed over the years, first by uncontrolled tree growth and Victorian bedding, and later by tarmac roads. Visitors and promenaders have had to wait for the recent restoration to experience Nash's Pavilion fully integrated with its setting.

The grounds have now been restored to incorporate Nash's serpentine drive which curves from the William IV Gate towards the Dome and continues over the western lawn to a carriage-turning circle in front of the porte cochère. Irregular beds of mixed shrubs and flowers border the winding paths and drives with the intervals between them disclosing to the visitor a varying succession of views.

The accounts for the Royal Pavilion gardens were discovered by Jessica Rutherford in the Public Records Office; apart from documenting the entire construction of the garden, they list every tree and shrub variety supplied for

the grounds. For the most part herbaceous plants were only specified by quantity, not unfortunately by name. All the trees and shrubs used in the newly-restored gardens are known to have been introduced into England before 1825. The choice of bulbs and herbaceous plants is more difficult, however, as after 150 years of hybridization it is harder to identify exact modern equivalents to Regency varieties. Therefore the closest in form and colour have been chosen. After several years the shrubs and trees have matured to reflect Nash's original picturesque scheme. (See Guide to the Royal Pavilion Estate & the Gardens pp.74–79)

ABOVE LEFT: *A section of the serpentine paths being restored; the Pavilion is still shrouded in scaffolding and blue protective plastic.*

ABOVE CENTRE: *Restoration commences around the porte cochère.*

ABOVE RIGHT: *The tarmac road being removed.*

BELOW: *The restored gardens to the west of the Pavilion.*

Guide to the Royal Pavilion Estate and the Gardens

Visitors to the Pavilion can now enjoy a walk around the Royal Pavilion Estate to view not only the restored Royal Pavilion (and related buildings) but also the gardens, reinstated to the original Regency scheme devised by John Nash.

Key to the plan

❶ As you leave the **Pavilion Shop** and turn right into Pavilion Buildings to face the present Indian (or South) Gate, you are standing by the site of the range of Pavilion buildings that contained servants' quarters, subsidiary kitchens and other ancillary facilities for the Royal Household. These formed a substantial block of buildings which extended southwards to the current line of the buildings of North Street. Following the purchase of the Pavilion in 1850 these were demolished and replaced by a street of shops.

❷ **The Indian Gate** was the gift of the people of India, erected to commemorate the Indian soldiers wounded during the First World War who were tended in the military hospital established on the Royal Pavilion Estate. Between December 1, 1914, and February 15, 1916, over 4,000 Indian patients passed through the hospital. Substantial alterations were required for this purpose. In addition to the operating theatres nine kitchens of three different types were established: one for meat eating Hindus, one for Muslims and one for vegetarians, and each ward was equipped with two separate water supplies. The gateway was designed by Thomas Tyrwhitt in a simple Gujerati style and was unveiled by His Highness The Maharaja of Patiala on October 26, 1921. It replaced an earlier south gate erected by the Corporation following its acquisition of the Pavilion in 1850.

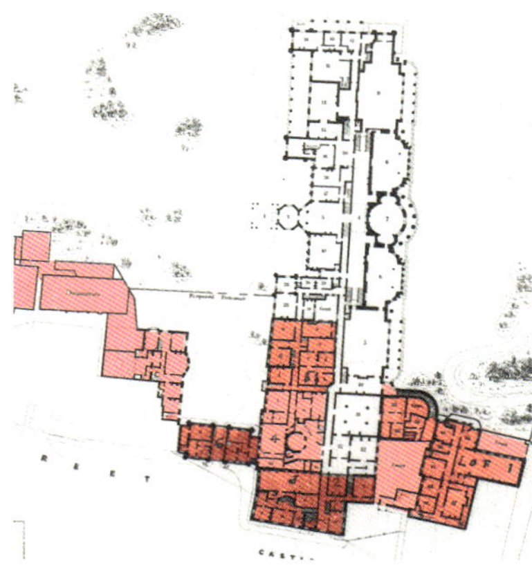

TOP: *Plan of the Royal Pavilion in 1849, showing the extent ofthe ancilary officers and servants Quarters.*

ABOVE: The Music Room as a Hospital for Indian Soldiers, *by C.H.H. Burleigh, c. 1915.*

BELOW: *The Indian Gateway completed in 1921, from a postcard made to commemorate the opening by H.H. The Maharaja of Patiala, October 1921.*

FAR LEFT: *Plan of the Estate, with key.*

The Grounds of the Royal Pavilion

When the Prince first came to stay in the farmhouse that was to be transformed into the Royal Pavilion the grounds were very different from their appearance today. The lodging house had little land attached to it. It was the gradual acquisition of surrounding land by the Prince of Wales that allowed the creation of the gardens you see today.

The Western Lawns were acquired over several decades. By 1795 the Prince's marriage to Caroline of Brunswick had eased his financial position sufficiently to allow the purchase of the Dairy Field, an area of land immediately to the north and west of the present Pavilion Buildings. As George's schemes grew more grandiose the desire to expand the Marine Pavilion required the demolition of the existing stabling. The new stables designed by William Porden, necessitated the acquisition of more land to the west. Gradually the parcels of land were united to form an estate.

In 1793 he and his neighbour, the Duke of Marlborough, paid to install a drain in the Steine in return for which they were allowed to enclose an area of the Steine as gardens for their properties. These areas are now essentially **The Eastern Lawns**.

The Pavilion grounds were first opened to the public on 29 June, 1850, when a range of by-laws were applied to prohibit smoking, intoxication, begging, games, and ragged or offensive attire. The present miniature stone balustrade to the east was installed in 1921–23. At the same time the eastern lawns were levelled and several pools installed.

ABOVE: *The west front of the Pavilion from the north west.*

ABOVE RIGHT: Interior of the Royal Stables, *designed by Porden, from* Nash's Views.

RIGHT: *View of the exterior of the Royal Stables (now the Dome Theatre), with the Riding House (now the Corn Exchange) to the left.*

❸ **The Royal Pavilion.** The complex composition of domes, towers and minarets of the building is characteristic of Nash's romantic style and clearly disguised the size of the Pavilion. Flanking the central large dome are seen two towers that serviced the interior rooms over the Saloon, one with a staircase, the other with a hoist. To achieve a picturesque effect the rendered surfaces of the Pavilion were lined out and painted in imitation of stone to create a unified vision of a building made of Bath stone.

Visitors can walk through the gardens by the perimeter path to view the spectacular **East Front.** Ingeniously the architect John Nash transformed Holland's modest structure with a grand central dome (over the Saloon), balanced by the sweeping tent roofs of the Music and Banqueting Rooms and a forest of small domes, minarets, pinnacles and chimney stacks. The exterior draws liberally on Indian architecture with the façade clothed in a delicate pierced stone screen.

❹ **The Site of the Ice House** was in the south-west corner of the grounds. This ice house, a domed, brick structure, had served the Pavilion since the 1790s (see p.61).

❺ **The Royal Stables** (now the Dome Theatre) were designed for the Prince of Wales by William Porden, who based his design on the Paris Corn Market. Financial difficulties delayed the project so that although the great domed roof, 80ft in diameter and 65ft high, was finished in 1804 the exterior was only finished in April 1805; the whole block, including the Riding House, was completed in 1808. The stables accommodated some sixty horses with quarters for ostlers and grooms off the first floor

galleries. In the centre of the floor was an octagonal pool and fountain for watering the horses. In 1821 an underground passageway was constructed from the King's new ground floor apartments to the stables and riding house to allow him direct and private access.

Following the purchase of the Estate by the town in 1850, the Stables and adjoining Riding Hall were let as cavalry barracks from 1856 until 1864. In 1867 the Dome, as it had become known, was reconstructed as a concert hall.

The interior was drastically remodelled between 1934–35 by Robert Atkinson. The Dome remains in use today as a concert hall and conference venue.

❻ **The Porte Cochère** was added to the Dome in 1901 and is now the entrance to the Museum & Art Gallery (see ❿ p.78).

❼ **The Riding House** (now the Corn Exchange), adjacent to the Stables, was also designed by William Porden and built between 1803–8.

In 1868 it acquired its present name when it became the venue for the weekly corn market. It was also altered by Atkinson between 1934–37 with a new entrance provided in Church Street which has a canopied doorway dominated by a large figure of Ceres, the goddess of corn, by the sculptor James Woodford.

❽ **The William IV** or **North Gate** was designed for William IV in 1832 by the architect Joseph Good. Appointed architect to the Royal Pavilion ten years earlier, Good also designed the South Lodge, together with dormitories and stabling on the estate, all of which were later demolished.

To the east stands Sir Francis Chantrey's statue of George IV which was paid for by a public subscription which raised 3,000 guineas. It was unveiled on its original site in the Steine on 9 October, 1828, and was moved here in 1922 to allow for the erection of the town's war memorial.

❾ Adjacent to the Gate itself stands **North Gate House**. This is now the only remaining house of Marlborough Row, a terrace of nine houses which extended southwards towards the Pavilion. North Gate House remains complete with oriental additions of turrets and scalloped arches added by Good to harmonise with his gatehouse.

TOP: Interior of the Riding House *(now the Corn Exchange) designed by Porden, from Nash's* Views.

ABOVE: *Detail of the North Gate. Built in 1832 for William IV the gate fulfilled George IV's wish for a magnificent northern entrance to the Pavilion grounds.*

⑩ The Museum & Art Gallery

A museum collection had been commenced in the early 1850s. With the acquisition in 1861 of the Brighton Royal Literary and Scientific Institution's collection, it soon outgrew the few rooms it occupied in the Pavilion. A Museum, Art Gallery and Library were built in 1873 to the Moorish designs of the Borough Surveyor, Philip Lockwood. The site was originally intended to be used as tennis courts for Queen Adelaide but had been in use for many years as an area of auxiliary stabling.

Substantial additions were made in 1901–2 to house a lending library. The Museum possesses extensive collections of fine and decorative arts, World art, costume, local history and archaeology (admission free).

RIGHT: *Interior of Brighton Museum & Art Gallery. The large central space was built as a picture gallery in 1873. It now houses the Museum's collection of twentieth-century art and design.*

FAR RIGHT: *Detail of restored beds with Purple Loosestrife* (Lythrum salicaria), *Hydrangea* (Hydrangea arborescens) *and Mallow* (Lavatera olbia).

Guide to the planting scheme in the Gardens

The gardens are laid out according to John Nash's plan of the early 1820s, with the sinuous flowery shrubberies typical of the Regency period. This style evolved from the more natural, fluid forms created with trees and shrubs in eighteenth-century English landscape gardening which replaced the formal French-inspired *parterres* of the seventeenth century.

The rules for the design of shrubberies were described in two books written by Henry Phillips, a local landscape gardener who planted part of the Kemp Town estate in 1828. The accounts for the construction of the Royal Pavilion gardens begin in 1816. They record the number and species of all the plants delivered by John Willmott's Lewisham nursery, although sadly there are no planting plans. The restored shrubberies reflect these two sources; they contain examples of nearly all the species mentioned in the nursery bills, while the plant associations follow Henry Phillips's instructions. Some beds on the east lawn were planted in the mid-1980s, the remainder in 1993.

A well-planted shrubbery, writes Phillips, must depend upon contrasting shades of green for its permanent effect as 'underplanted flowers are of shorter duration'. He recommended planting laurel, both common and Portuguese, myrtle, box, privet, tamarisk and variegated hollies and ivies. These form the green structure of the borders, particularly those which screen roads and other twentieth-century intrusions. When these shrubs and the new trees have reached a good height, honeysuckle, vines, clematis and nasturtiums will be grown up the stems to create 'natural festoons of wilderness scenery'.

Phillips' shrubberies also depended upon 'the selection of trees and shrubs which succeed each other in blossoming throughout the year or on fruits which ornament them'.

In early Spring look for flowering almond trees, fragrant *Daphne odora* and *Daphne mezereon*, single and double flowered gorse, red-flowered heath (*Erica mediterranea*), *Camellia*, Japanese Quince (*Chaenomeles*), *Magnolia tripetala* and Jews Mallow (*Kerria japonica*). Snowdrops, Primroses, Wild Daffodils and winter Hellebores should be in bloom at the front of shrubberies and Yellow Crocus on the east lawn.

In May look for double pink Hawthorn blossom, Persian, Chinese and common Lilacs (*Syringa persica, S. chinensis* and *S. vulgaris*) with Guelder Rose (*Viburnum opulus*), flowering underneath Laburnum trees; mounds of Spanish Broom (*Genista hispanica*), Purple Broom (*Cytisus purpureus*), Pink Bridewort (*Spirea salicifolia*), clumps of Tulips and, at the front of shrubberies, Periwinkle (*Vinca minor* and *major*), evergreen Candytuft (*Iberis sempervirens*), yellow Daisies of Leopards Bane (*Doronicum orientale*), Forget-me-nots (*Myosotis*) and, later in the month, scented yellow day Lilies (*Hemerocallis flava*) and the double crimson Peony (*Paeonia officinalis rubra plena*).

In the following Summer months look for many varieties of pink and white flowered Rock Rose (*Cistus*), yellow pea-flowered Common Broom (*Spartium junceum*), Rosemary, Grey-leaved Cotton Lavender, Jasmin (*Jasminum humile Revolutum*), Mock Orange (*Philadelphus coronarius*), yellow-flowered Potentilla (*Potentilla fruticosa*), St John's Wort (*Hypericum prolificum* and *H. androsaemum*) Rose-acacia (*Robinia hispida*) and fifteen varieties of old roses! The herbaceous plants peeping out from among the greenery will include more Peonies, Hollyhocks, Foxgloves, Sweet Williams, blue Larkspurs and Love-in-a-mist (*Nigella*), scarlet Poppies (*Papaver bracteatum*), double Daisies, Columbines, Pinks (*Dianthus* Bat's Double Red and *Dianthus* Old Salmon Clove), Sweet Rocket (*Hesperis matronalis*) scarlet Maltese Cross (*Lychnis chalcedonica*).

In the late Summer and early Autumn the following plants can be seen at their best: Strawberry Trees (*Arbutus unedo*) with both flowers and fruit, Hydrangeas (*H. quercifolia*, *H. arborescens* and *Hydrangeas* 'Joseph Banks'), Fuchsia (*Fuchsia magellanica*), Tree Hollyhock (*Hibiscus syriacus*), Witch Hazel (*Hamamelis virginiana*), *Abelia grandiflora* and Yellow Late Broom (*Cytisus nigricans*). Herbaceous plants include Rudbeckias, Golden Rod (*Solidago canadensis*), Tiger Lilies (*Lilium tigrinum*), Bears Breeches, (*Acanthus spinosus*), Sunflowers (*Helenium autumnale*). Chrysanthemums, China Asters and Michaelmas Daisies. Many of these plants will flower until the first severe winter frosts when visitors can still enjoy a promenade through the gardens to see the colour in Hollies, *Pyracantha*, Snowberries and Coral Berries (*Symphoricarpos*), red Dogwood stems (*Cornus*), spiky Yuccas and Phormiums, Silver Birch, winter flowering Heathers (*Erica carnea*) and Laurustinus (*Viburnum tinus*).

Brief Bibliography

Books

Aldrich, Megan (Ed.), *The Craces, Royal Decorators 1768–1899*, London, 1990.

de Bellaigue, G., Harris, J., and Millar, O., *Buckingham Palace*, London, 1968.

Brayley, E.W., *Illustrations of Her Majesty's Palace at Brighton*, London, 1838.

Collard, Frances, *Regency Furniture*, Woodbridge, 1985.

Dinkel, John, *The Royal Pavilion, Brighton*, London, 1983.

Jackson-Stops, G., *Views of the Royal Pavilion*, reprint of Nash's *Views* with a commentary, London, 1991.

Morley, John, *The Making of the Royal Pavilion*, London, 1984.

Musgrave, Clifford, *Royal Pavilion, An Episode in the Romantic*, London, 1951. *Regency Furniture*, London, 1961.

Nash, John, *Views of the Royal Pavilion, Brighton*, 1826 (published 1827).

Roberts, Henry, *A History of the Royal Pavilion*, London, 1939.

Rutherford, JMF *A Prince's Passion: The Life of the Royal Pavilion*, Brighton, 2003.

Articles

Batey, M., 'Regency setting restored', *Country Life*, 26 April, 1984 (on the Royal Pavilion garden restoration).

de Bellaigue, G., 'George IV: his approach to furniture', *Furniture History Society Journal*, 1985.

Rogers, Julian, 'The approach to the restoration of the Music Room, Brighton Pavilion, following arson in 1975', *The Conservator*, no.4, 1980, UKIC.

Rutherford, J. M. F., 'The Great Kitchen, Royal Pavilion', *Country Life*, 14 December, 1989.

Rutherford, J. M. F., 'Redecoration and restoration: The Crace Firm at the Royal Pavilion 1863–1900', Aldrich, *op. cit.*

Rutherford, J. M. F., '"As full of lamps as Hancock's Shop": lighting in the Royal Pavilion 1815–1900', *Country House Lighting*, Temple Newsam, Leeds, 1992.

The Friends of the Royal Pavilion, Art Gallery & Museums, Brighton

Patron: H.R.H. The Prince of Wales

The Friends support the restoration and preservation of the Royal Pavilion and the gardens, as well as new projects in Brighton & Hove's other Museums.

If you would like further details and an application form, please contact the Royal Pavilion, Brighton, East Sussex, BN1 1EE or telephone 01273 290900. royalpavilion@brighton-hove.gov.uk

Acknowledgements

The Royal Pavilion is a unique and extraordinary building that, since its creation, has both inspired and irritated, engendering enthusiasm or disdain in the visitor, but never indifference. J. W. Croker's claim in 1818 that it was 'an absurd waste of money and will be a ruin in half a century or sooner …' fortunately proved to be ill-founded. Its preservation was largely due to the enlightened attitude of certain civic leaders in Brighton and numerous generous benefactors over the last 150 years.

Since 1850 the Pavilion has undergone successive phases of redecoration and restoration. Most recently, the entire structure was restored over a twelve-year period, funded by Brighton & Hove City Council with invaluable support from English Heritage. The first floor bedrooms have been reinstated and refurbished to their Regency appearance. The gardens, the picturesque setting for the Pavilion, have been returned to the layout and planting schemes designed by John Nash.

The Royal Pavilion is owned, managed and funded by Brighton & Hove City Council. The continuing support of the Council allows us to care for this building, open it to the public, and pass it on to the next generation.

We are particularly grateful to the following benefactors for their generous support and assistance with the restoration of the interior of the Royal Pavilion: G. P. & J. Baker Limited; Brunschwig & Fils; His Grace the 11th Duke of Devonshire; The Friends of the Royal Pavilion, Art Gallery and Museums; Heal & Son Limited; Christopher Howe; The Leche Trust; George and Martin Levy; The Regency Society of Brighton and Hove The Coral Samuel Charitable Trust; The L. J. Skaggs and Mary C. Skaggs Foundation; Smith & Watson Inc; the Dmitro Trust; His Grace the Duke of Wellington and many individuals who prefer to remain anonymous. H.M. The Queen has most kindly lent additional items of furniture and objects to refurbish newly restored rooms.

The continuing restoration of the Royal Pavilion gardens would not have been possible without the support of The Ian Askew Charitable Trust; The John Coates Charitable Trust; East Sussex County Council; English Heritage; The Esmée Fairbairn Charitable Trust; The Friends of the Royal Pavilion, Art Gallery and Museums; John G. MacCarthy and The Historic Gardens Trust (Sussex); The Hove and Brighton Urban Conservation Project; The Ernest Kleinwort Charitable Trust, and The Priory Charitable Trust.

The research and design of the reconstructed scheme, and the supervision of the planting contract, was carried out by the Landscape Group of East Sussex County Council Planning Department, with Virginia Hinze as landscape architect and Ken Nice as technician. Further assistance and advice were generously given by Roger Murton, Mavis Batey and Marion Waller.